W9-BNH-353

Jim J. Yuen

Inspecting
A Home
OR Income
Property

🔟
Ten Speed Press

1☉
TEN SPEED PRESS
P.O. Box 7123
Berkeley, California 94707

Cover and book design by Nancy Austin
Composition by The Recorder Typesetting Network

Library of Congress Cataloging-in-Publication Data

Yuen, Jim.
  Inspecting a home or income property.

  Bibliography: p.
  Includes index.
  1. Dwellings—Inspection.   I. Title.
TH4817.5.Y84 1986   643′.12   86-6050
ISBN 0-89815-184-8

Printed in the United States of America

2 3 4 5 — 93 92 91 90

Contents

Preface

During twenty-four years of inspecting residential and income properties, I have found that most prospective home buyers and real estate investors as well as many real estate salespeople are not sufficiently well informed to make prudent evaluations of the physical condition of houses or apartment buildings. On their pre-purchase visits to a property they simply do not know what to look for or how to interpret what they see.

Inspecting a Home or Income Property is designed to help home buyers, investors, and real estate agents make thorough and intelligent pre-purchase inspections of residential and income properties. The book explains the how, what, where, when, and why of comprehensive inspection procedures that will enable readers to identify existing and potential structural, electrical, plumbing, and mechanical problems. The probable causes of such problems and their likely solutions are also discussed.

We have all heard the phrase "buyer beware." Reading this book will allow buyers to become aware enough to exercise appropriate caution. Furthermore, "buyer beware" is no longer a sufficient rationale for real estate agents. Recent court decisions have held real estate licensees increasingly responsible for the discovery and disclosure of all relevant property defects. Although real estate personnel need not become expert building inspectors or engineers, they are expected to make every reasonable effort to inform buyers and sellers of the physical condition of properties being traded.

Finally, in the course of explaining property inspection procedures, this book provides a wealth of information about residential safety. For a thorough pre-purchase inspection can save prospective property owners from both the unpleasant surprises of unanticipated repair bills and also from dangers to health and welfare posed by unsafe physical conditions.

Acknowledgments

I'm very grateful to my colleagues and friends who assisted me with the development of this edition of *Inspecting a Home or Income Property*. This book would not have been possible without the help and support of the following individuals:

Scott Atkinson	For his editorial assistance
Randy Blair	Entomologist
Ralph Carrillo	Chief building inspector
Fred B. Cullum	Certified combination inspector; Director: California Building Officials; building official, City of San Mateo; instructor—building codes and related technologies
Jim Devine	City of San Mateo Building Department, for floor plan illustration
Laurence M. Kornfield	Certified building official, certified building inspector, and licensed general contractor
Stanley Low	Land-use specialist
Robert L. Rider	For his editorial assistance and consultation
Ken Tom	For his illustrations
Roderic C. Tosetti	Electrical consultant; electrical contractor; instructor—building technologies, College of San Mateo

Inspecting A Home Or Income Property

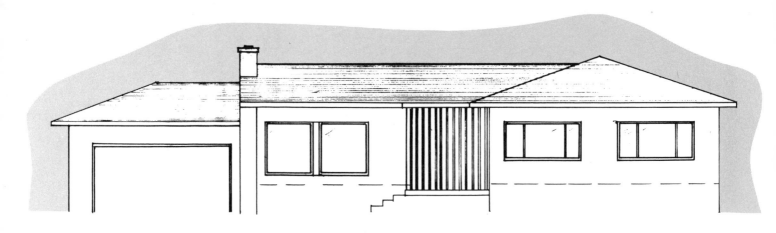

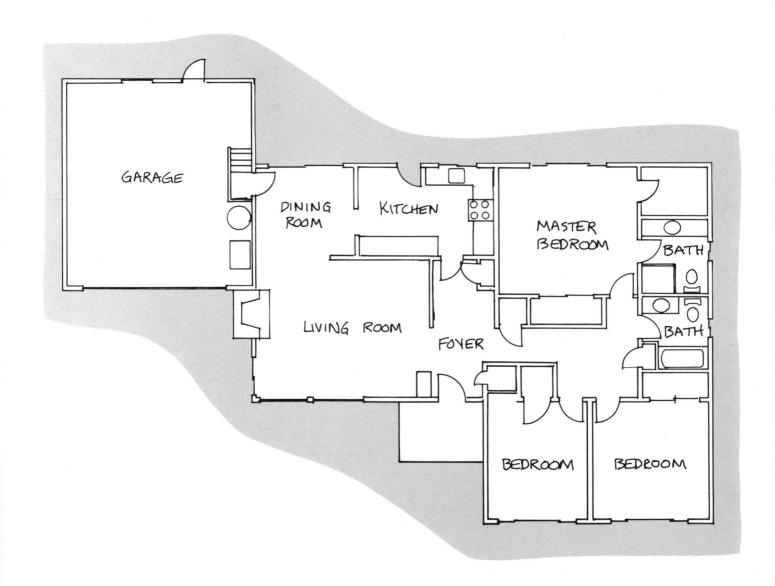

1

How a thorough inspection can save home buyers and investors dollars, costly litigation, and potential hazards to property and can save realtors the revocation of their real estate licenses

The Fundamentals of Inspection

A complete inspection will cover the roof, foundation, plumbing, electrical and mechanical systems, walls, ceilings, floors, appliances, safety devices, security requirements, nonconforming additions to existing property, and much more.

Over the years, I have been involved with friends, relatives, real estate licensees, and consumers who have purchased homes unaware of existing problems such as nonconforming additions of family rooms, illegal wiring, or new roofs installed by nonprofessional personnel.

A leaking roof, wiring violations, and leaky plumbing under the house are usually detected by the new property owners after the close of escrow. That's the time when the new owners may wish to sue the real estate agent or previous owners, if the problems are not remedied. State departments of real estate are becoming more aware of real estate licensees who are not revealing to new buyers the known facts and problems of the properties they are selling. If proven in court that an agent misrepresented the facts as known, the department of real estate will revoke or suspend the agent's license.

A pre-sale inspection by a professional and impartial inspector is one way to avoid problems among agents, home buyers, investors, owners, consumers, and others involved in property sales. A pre-sale inspection not only identifies existing or potential problems but allows for viable and inexpensive ways to correct and prevent future problems as well.

Professional Housing Inspectors vs. Building Inspectors

Building inspectors are employees of your local government who are responsible for making sure that all structural, electrical, plumbing, and mechanical alterations to buildings meet the relevant local codes. If you request a building inspector to make a pre-sale inspection, almost all the information about the premises will become part of the official record. An independent housing inspector, in contrast, will prepare an inspection report for your eyes only. Furthermore, the independent housing inspector's primary responsibility is to protect you. For a fee that is typically between $175 and $400, a competent inspector will meticulously check all the basic components of the property and record his findings in a comprehensive report.

To derive the maximum benefit from an inspector's services, you should walk through the house with him. This will assist you in making your evaluation, interpreting the written report, and checking your own assessment against that of a trained observer.

An independent inspector's checklist should include an evaluation of the quality and condition of each of the following:

- Grading, drainage, landscaping, fences, paved areas, retaining walls, recreational facilities, garage.
- Exterior walls (including insulation), doors, windows, porches, decks, steps.
- Roofing materials and construction, vents, hatches, skylights, gutters, downspouts, chimneys.
- Crawl space or basement—construction, settlement, water penetration, termite or rot damage.
- Attic—access, ventilation, insulation, signs of leakage, fire safety.
- Interior—walls, floors, ceilings, fireplace or stove, stairs closets, fire safety.
- Electrical system.
- Plumbing system.
- Heating and cooling systems.
- Kitchen and bathrooms.

Although rating systems vary, the report should clearly indicate the relative condition of each item and whether repair or replacement is necessary.

Location of Property

The most important consideration in purchasing residential or income property is location. Some factors to be considered are:

- proximity to schools and place of employment.
- accessibility to shopping areas, recreational facilities, and public transportation.
- neighborhood traffic patterns.

Take a leisurely stroll around the area during different times of the day to get a general feel of the neighborhood. Try to talk to some of the people you meet on your walks.

Families with school-age children are primarily concerned about the location of grammar, secondary, and high schools. Besides asking about the proximity of schools, inquire about the quality of education offered compared to schools in adjacent districts, the possibility of school closures in light of population changes, the possibility of changes in school boundaries, and the likelihood of busing.

A consideration of equal or greater importance for most home buyers is the proximity of the house to their places of employment. Both the distance from work and local commute patterns are relevant.

Points to be considered in terms of daily living include the ease with which one can get to the nearest supermarket; the whereabouts of the closest parks, libraries, public swimming pools, and other recreational facilities; and, especially if there is only one car in the family, the accessibility to public transportation. Families with school-age children will also want to know about traffic patterns on nearby streets at different times of day: Are there too many highly traveled streets for parents to feel at ease when their children are playing outside or walking to friends' houses?

Also find out about nearby hospitals, medical facilities, and police and fire stations. Proximity to local industries and airports may be an issue for people worried about pollution or noise.

How to Prepare for a Pre-Sale Inspection

Researching the history of a property is a very worthwhile and valuable part of the inspection procedure whether the property is brand new or fifty years old.

Every building is identified by an assessor's parcel number (usually nine digits) or the address of the parcel; for example, 012-345-678 or 123 A Street, Anytown.

Step 1. Contact the local assessor's office by telephone or in person. If in person, obtain a written authorization from the owners of the property. Some cities/counties will copy the street file for you. A copy can be useful in case disagreements arise about the history of the building.

All assessor's information is public information unless otherwise specified by the county assessor. Building permits are usually documented in the assessor's record. But don't assume that a permit on file has been given final approval by the building department. The permit could have expired before the work was completed.

Step 2. Go to the local building department and ask to check the files for outstanding complaints and building permits (whether active or completely expired). Ask if other divisions or departments (planning and zoning, for example) have outstanding permits on the property.

Some building departments may offer inspection service for the purpose of checking properties for code violations. If they do make an inspection, however, the current owner of the property may be liable for correcting violations whether the property is sold or not.

Step 3. Check with the local health department to determine whether any outstanding complaints are on file. This step is important if the property is an apartment building with three or more units.

Step 4. Contact the local water department to determine the normal water pressure for the property. Water pressure is expressed in pounds per square inch (psi) and normal water pressure is usually between 55 psi and 65 psi. Higher water pressure is not recommended because it causes the loss of considerable amounts of water, banging noises in the water pipes, wear and tear on the washer stems of the faucets, and potential damage to clothes and dishwashers. A pressure regulator should be installed if pressure exceeds 80 psi.

Low water pressure may be the result of corrosion or sediment in pipes. If that is the case, the pipes may need to be replaced. If the owner of the property states that new copper pipes were recently installed, but a pressure test of the main service hose bibb shows that the water pressure is 40 psi or less, ask the water department to inspect the city's main pipe connection to the home to determine if the city water pipe is defective.

Also ask if the water is hard or soft. Hard water has excessive amounts of minerals such as calcium and magnesium but a water softener may be added to the home's water supply to reduce hardness.

Step 5. Contact the local utility service if any gas-fired appliance appears to not be working properly. Ask the gas company to verify that the appliance has been connected properly. If an appliance is found to be defective or hazardous, the gas company will disconnect it and will reconnect it only when the owner has repaired or replaced the appliance to code. Inspections by the gas company are usually free, but they usually will not inspect electrical appliances.

Step 6. Obtain a reputable and reliable pest control firm to make an inspection of the property. (On pest control reports, see Chapter 7.)

Step 7. Ask your local building or planning department for any relevant soil reports. These reports, filed by government soil or civil engineers, will mention the soil type, the level of the water table, and the condition of the building's foundation.

Step 8. If the property is in an earthquake zone, you will want to find out how close it is to any active faults, how stable the underlying soils are, and how "quake proof" the building is. Check with the U.S. Geological Survey office. The age of the building usually determines which earthquake safety measures were included in the construction. For example, a house built with a brick foundation without adequate bracing for the walls and ceilings will crumble or fall apart if the earth movement is great. A building constructed in accordance with today's building code requirements would likely sustain far less damage. Newer buildings have many features designed to prevent serious injury and property damage: a reinforced continuous foundation; bracing of walls, ceilings, exterior decks, etc; strapping for the water heater; fastening of heavy appliances to the floor; and anchoring of tall bookshelves to the wall.

Four Categories of Inspection

To conduct a proper inspection you need to know what to look for, where to look, and when to enlist the services of a professional.

A comprehensive residential inspection has four major components: structural, electrical, plumbing, and mechanical. The chapters that follow deal with each of these areas and provide a brief summary of common problems, their causes, consequences, and resolutions.

Of course, this book will *not* train you as a building or housing inspector. But it will familiarize you with the qualities of a well-designed inspection.

Caveat for real estate personnel: If you think that a property has a defect, it is incumbent upon you to refer your client, the owner or buyer, to an appropriate expert or specialist who can give a reliable opinion or judgment.

Fig. 1 presents a suggested list of equipment to bring when you make your formal inspection of a property.

Special Attention:
Areas Most Vulnerable to Lawsuits

Property owners are particularly vulnerable to lawsuits if accidents or injuries occur on their premises. All the following items are discussed in their proper place later in this book, but it is worth giving this checklist special attention before and during your inspection.

☐ *Stairs and handrails.* The most common accidents are related to tripping or falling on stairs. Property owners are expected to keep interior and exterior stairs in good repair as well as to meet all current codes regarding guardrails, handrails, tread type, and so on.

☐ *Elevator maintenance.* If the building has a public elevator, it must be inspected by local or state authorities at least once a year. Defects that occur during everyday use should be repaired promptly. For example, the failure of an elevator to stop even with the base of the floor could cause people to trip or fall.

☐ *Swimming pool area.* A minimum four-foot high fence with a self-closing gate is required. There should be adequate protection against unauthorized use of the pool: A posted No Swimming sign may not be enough to discourage outsiders. The swimming pool area must have a non-slip surface; outdoor electrical outlets should be protected and grounded; depth markers should be clearly visible; and lights and filters should be in good working order.

☐ *Gas-fired appliances.* All gas-fired appliances must be properly vented. Floor furnaces always pose a potential hazard, since toddlers may crawl over the hot floor grille and barefoot adults inadvertently may walk on it. Paper and combustibles should be stored well away from appliances and vents.

☐ *Water heaters.* Water heaters whose pressure-relief valves are malfunctioning or are improperly piped can explode or send scalding water all over residents.

☐ *Glass doors.* Glass shower-enclosure doors and patio or deck sliding glass doors must be made of shatterproof tempered safety glass (can be laminated safety glazing or may be acrylic or other plastic material).

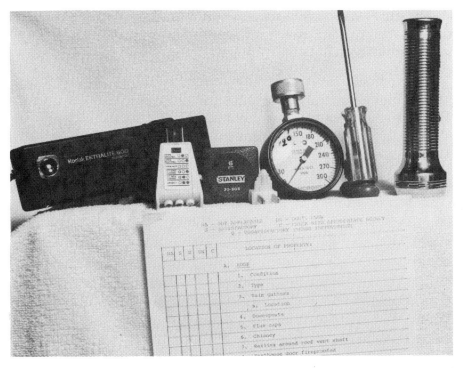

Figure 1

Tools for inspection

Left to right:

Camera	$25–$50
*Circuit analyzer	$8
Tape measure	$4
Night light	$2
Water gauge	$6
Screwdriver	$9
Flashlight	$3

Additional tools:

Level	$7
Ladder, preferably an extension ladder	$50–$125
Step ladder (for attic access)	$50

A circuit analyzer will enable you to detect whether the polarity at an electrical outlet is correct and whether the ground is properly wired and functioning (see Chapter 3).

☐ *Pest control.* Property owners are responsible for retaining the services of licensed pest control companies to eradicate cockroaches, fleas, mice, rats, and similar critters. Toddlers and small children are very vulnerable to flea, rat, and mouse bites. Cockroaches can cause contamination of food products.

☐ *Grounds maintenance.* Property owners can be held liable for accidents resulting from overgrown shrubbery, fallen branches, broken glass on walkways, overgrown tree roots, etc.

☐ *Hazardous combustibles.*   Combustible materials must not be stored near gas-fired heaters or furnaces or other unsuitable areas.

☐ *Illegal additions and fly-by-night repairs.*   Owners are legally liable for any accidents involving any illegal additions or fly-by-night repairs of electrical, plumbing, mechanical, or structural work.

☐ *Smoke detectors.*   Most jurisdictions require that smoke detectors be installed in private homes upon sale, transfer, or remodeling of the house. Similarly, many jurisdictions require that all rental properties have smoke detectors in the hallways and in the individual units.

☐ *Asbestos.*   Asbestos was widely used between the 1940s and early 1970s as fireproofing on ceilings and as insulation on pipes and boilers. Exposure to asbestos is now known to cause serious lung diseases and several kinds of cancer. Asbestos can be removed only by a technician certified by the federal Environmental Protection Agency (EPA). If you see chalky white paper wrapped around a furnace or heat ducts, *do not disturb the material.* Contact the EPA or the local office of the federal or state Occupational Safety and Health Administration (OSHA). A certified specialist will take air samples and advise you on how to proceed.

☐ *Formaldehyde.*   Formaldehyde compounds are continually used in items like bonding material, such as plywood or particle boards. Hazardous or toxic gases have been shown to be emitted into the air inside a building from some of these products. Other binder glues and construction products, as well as new furniture or rugs, may cause a serious toxic hazard in new buildings. The problem is particularly acute in homes where windows are usually kept closed and the air is restricted. Urea-formaldehyde is sometimes used as insulating material in building exterior walls although its use is now restricted in many states.

☐ *Radon.*   Radon is an odorless, tasteless, radioactive gas. It is the end product of the natural breaking down of uranium. If radon is present outdoors, there is very little health risk due to the dilution of radon in the atmosphere. If present indoors, there is a risk of higher concentrations due to the enclosed spaces in a building (which depend on the age and construction of the building and amount of radon in the soil). Radon gas usually enters a building from underlying soil through openings or cracks in the floor, concrete, walls, and drains in the floor. To help lessen the concentration of radon in your home, inspect it for adequate ventilation via windows, operable exhaust fans, and cross ventilation in the foundation crawl space. The major health problem in relation to radon is the possibility of lung cancer. For further information regarding radon, contact your state Radiation Protection Agency, or the federal Environmental Protection Agency.

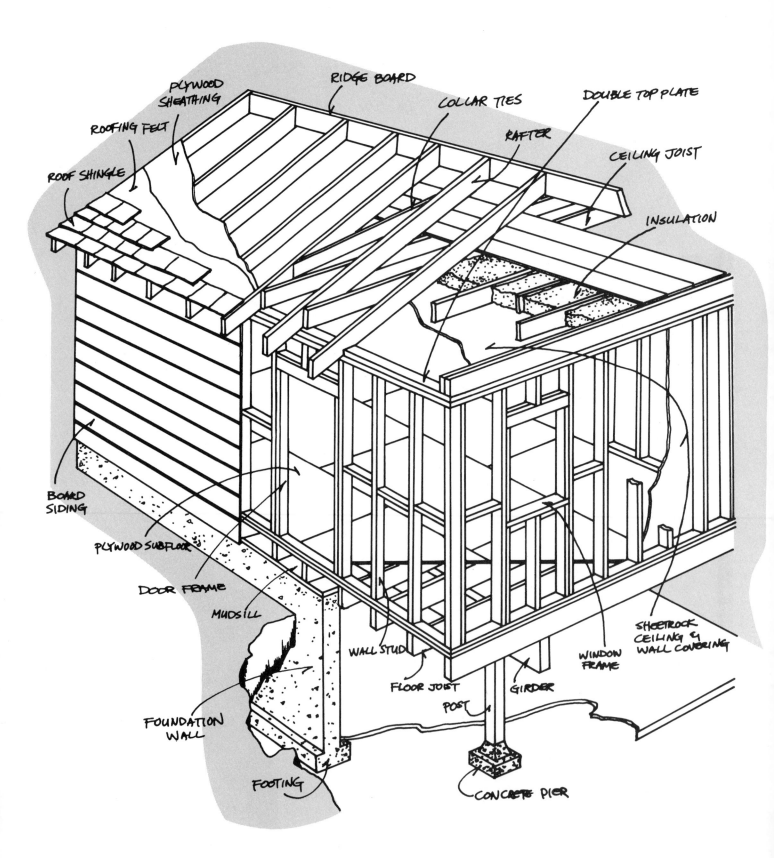

PLYWOOD SHEATHING

RIDGE BOARD

COLLAR TIES

DOUBLE TOP PLATE

ROOFING FELT

RAFTER

CEILING JOIST

ROOF SHINGLE

INSULATION

BOARD SIDING

PLYWOOD SUBFLOOR

DOOR FRAME

MUDSILL

WALL STUD

FLOOR JOIST

GIRDER

WINDOW FRAME

SHEETROCK CEILING & WALL COVERING

POST

FOUNDATION WALL

FOOTING

CONCRETE PIER

2

The Structure & Substructure

T he structural adequacy of any building is of primary importance. Because the foundation walls, floors, and roof have to withstand wind and earthquake loads, building codes always stipulate minimum construction requirements that builders must meet.

A thorough structural inspection must include an examination and evaluation of each of the following:

Foundation

Floor framing

Wall framing

Crawl space

Exterior walls

Fireplaces

Windows

Exterior doors

Roof and ceiling framing

Attic area

Roofing materials

Skylights

Chimneys

Gutters and downspouts

Insulation

Interior walls and ceilings

Interior floors

Stairways

Porches and decks

Garage

Drainage

Accessory buildings

Figure 2

Opposite:
Structural skeleton of a one-story house.

Overview: How a House Is Built

Fig. 2 presents a structural overview of a typical house.

The house foundation is excavated into the soil at least 12 inches deep, below the weaker topsoil, to provide a secure anchoring and avoid shifting.

Floor joists or girders are nailed to the mudsill (a wooden support above the foundation), which is in turn bolted to the foundation. This gives the base of the house (foundation and floor) a structural integrity that can resist earthquake and wind loads.

The walls are then erected on a sole plate and capped with a double top-plate. The top-plate links all the walls together and acts as a support for the ceiling joists and rafters, or for the second floor joists in a two-story house. Where openings occur at doors and windows, the loads from above are supported by beams called headers or lintels.

The roof is supported on the double top-plate. The pitch of the roof exerts outward pressure at the top of the supporting walls. To reduce this pressure, which would spread the walls and flatten the roof, collar ties are nailed from one rafter to another.

Houses built in earthquake zones have braces of solid wall sheeting that keep the walls from buckling and turn the whole structure into a very strong box.

Figure 3

First stage in constructing a building is digging of raw land.

Figure 4
Poured foundation.

Foundation

Exterior walls should be supported by an undamaged, continuous masonry foundation—either perimeter footings and walls or a concrete slab.

Most foundations for wood-floor houses are called spread footings. Spread footings are dug into the ground and spread the load of the house over the soil. Since soil is compressible to a certain extent, the footing will be wider for a two-story house than for a single-story building.

The typical depth of footing for a single-story house is 12 inches below grade; 18 inches below grade for a two-story, and 24 inches for a three-story building (Figs. 3 and 4).

Most building codes do not require reinforcing steel for foundations, so a certain amount of shrinkage cracking is normal. If the cracks are v-shaped, the foundation is undergoing differential settlement or heaving. Differential settlement occurs when the weight of the house is not uniformly distributed around the footing or where some areas of the supporting soil are weaker than others. Heaving occurs when expansive soil (such as adobe) gets wet and the increase in soil volume raises the foundation or cracks the concrete slabs.

A concrete slab should be 3-1/2 to 4 inches thick. Slab under living areas should be underlain with a moisture-proof membrane. If you notice a musty smell or mildewed carpets or walls in the house, new moisture-proofing may be needed. A standard test is to tape a small square of plastic sheeting to the slab for a few days. If water collects on the underside, the slab is seeping moisture.

As with perimeter foundations, hairline cracks in slabs are acceptable, but deep cracks and severe cracking call for further investigation by a foundation contractor or engineering firm (Fig. 5).

Figure 5

Top: *Cross-section through a standard "T" foundation.*

Bottom: *A concrete slab foundation with no separation between the soil and the underfloor.*

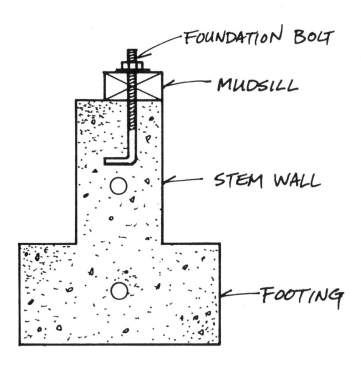

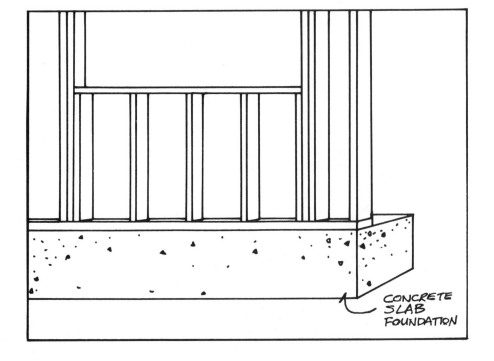

Soil Conditions

While the spread footings illustrated in this book are very common throughout the United States, local soil conditions may necessitate other types of footings.

One of the most common problem soils is adobe, or "popcorn" soil. Adobe is a highly expansive clay that has little strength when compressed (as by the weight of a house). Clayey soil when wet exerts upward pressure on the house foundation and causes cracking and heaving of garage slabs and driveways.

Solutions to an expansive soil condition include:

- Floating slabs—where a reinforced slab is poured on top of the ground and the weight of the house is distributed over the entire area of the house.

- Pier and grade beam foundations—where piers are drilled into the ground and concrete is poured into the holes and a reinforced concrete beam is laid to span the piers.

- Deep, narrow footings—which extend through the highly expansive and unstable topsoil.

Even with moisture conditioning the soil will expand and contract with seasonal changes. Existing cracks will widen, then shrink; doors will stick, then become loose. Do not attempt to correct these problems yourself: Any "repairs" may cause further damage.

Floor Framing

The mudsill is the 2″ × 4″ or 2″ × 6″ wood board (pressure treated or redwood only) that the floor joists rest on. In regions subject to earthquakes the mudsill should be bolted or otherwise secured to the foundation stem wall. These bolts or straps should be between 32 and 72 inches apart, within 12 inches from the end of the board.

The floor joists are designed to support the weight of furniture, appliances, and people. Some floor joists provide a rather bouncy floor—but this does not pose a structural problem. Floor joists are usually 2 inches wide and are spaced between 12 and 24 inches on center. (*On center* refers to the distance between the center axes of neighboring beams of wood.) Permitted spans vary with the kind and grade of wood. Typical spans for #2 Douglas fir (a common West Coast construction type and grade) are given later in this chapter along with the spans for rafters (see Fig. 17).

Posts and girders may be used to reduce the span of the floor joists. The posts are usually supported on pyramid-shaped concrete blocks set in concrete in the underfloor area. Girders are thicker than floor joists, usually

Figure 6

Top: *Laid subfloor. 4″ × 6″ girders, heating ducts, and water piping are visible underneath subflooring.*

Bottom: *Framework of a home under construction.*

4″ × 6″s or 4″ × 8″s (Fig. 6). Most building codes require that there be at least 12 inches of clearance from the ground under the house to the girders and at least 18 inches of clearance to the floor joists. This clearance forms a crawl space that allows access to the underside of the house.

One specific design for wood floors uses no joists. Such a floor is made of 1-1/8-inch thick plywood that sits on 4″ × 6″ girders spaced 48 inches on center.

Wall Framing

One- and two-story walls are usually framed with vertical 2″ × 4″ wooden studs spaced between 16 and 24 inches on center. The first story of a three-story building is framed with 3″ × 4″ or 2″ × 6″ studs. In extremely cold climates all exterior walls may be framed with 2″ × 6″ material to allow for the installation of thicker insulation.

The outsides of the walls may be covered with exterior cement plaster (stucco), particle board products, or wood. The interior surfaces may be covered with sheetrock (gypsum wallboard), interior plaster, or wood.

Figure 7

Above: *An underfloor foundation access, located in hallway closet.*

Left: *Damaged foundation. Note hole beneath underfloor access opening. Mesh screen should be replaced with quarter-inch mesh.*

Crawl Space

A crawl space needs fresh air and sunlight to help prevent moisture buildup, so look for underfloor vents around the perimeter of the building near ground level (Fig. 7). Proper ventilation means about 1 square foot of opening for each 150 square feet of underfloor area. The openings should allow cross-ventilation.

Vents should be corrosion-resistant wire mesh with quarter-inch openings. If you find horizontal louvers—or no coverings at all—plan to install mesh screens. No vegetation or other material should block the vents.

Observe whether the ground is covered with concrete. Concrete, which deters rat harborage and termite infestation, is required in some areas. The underfloor area should be clean and free of debris.

Many older houses are built with very high crawl spaces. A short "pony" or "cripple" wall extends up from the foundation, and the first floor rests on top of this wall. In earthquake areas, pony walls must be securely anchored to the foundation and be thoroughly braced, usually by application of well-nailed plywood to the studs and other framing of the wall as well as to the mudsill (Fig. 8).

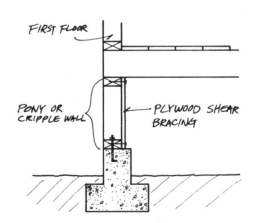

Figure 8

Proper bracing of a pony wall (cripple wall).

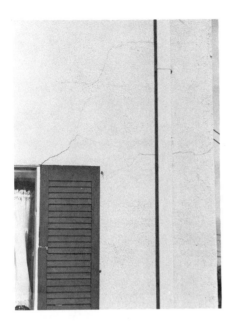

Figure 9

A stucco wall with numerous hairline cracks.

Figure 10

Paint peeling from stucco wall.

Exterior Walls

It is important to remember that a house is made up of tens of thousands of parts; that wood is a natural material subject to drying and shrinking, moistening and expanding, and, due to its grain, warping, twisting and cracking.

Given all that plus a foundation sitting on another natural material, the soil, cracks in the finishes of the building must be expected. Structural cracks: those that are 1/8 inch or more in width may justify contacting a local contractor for further investigation, but smaller cracks are best ignored or covered by wallpaper or panelling.

Sight down the walls from the side. Are they plumb or bowed out at the top? From a distance, do any walls seem to sag horizontally?

Now check the siding. Common types include stucco, solid lumber, plywood, aluminum, and vinyl.

Stucco. A finish usually comprises two or three coats of cement. The first (or "scratch") coat covers wire mesh and building paper attached to the wall studs. The second ("brown") and third ("color") coats are applied over the scratch coat. In many places, the scratch and the color coats are the same; in these instances you can "get by" with two coats.

A building covered with stucco will be subject to minor cracks, such as diagonal cracks running up from window or door corners (Fig. 9). If the walls are adequately papered and have a weep screed (metal channel at bottom of wall, minimum 6 inches from grade to allow moisture to escape from under stucco) at the bottom (most older buildings don't), any water entering the cracks will eventually channel downward and out. If there are no weep screeds, doublecheck the interior finish of the outside wall for evidence of moisture trapped behind the stucco.

Minor cracks can be patched using approved exterior stucco materials. Cracks wider than an eighth of an inch may indicate undue structural stress—consider contacting a local contractor for an expert opinion. Run your hand over the stucco; if paint chalks off easily, it is not adhering properly (Fig. 10).

Wood siding. Warping, dry rot, and peeling on wood siding and trim indicate inadequate weatherproofing. At best, these walls will need scraping, priming, and repainting (Fig. 11). Be sure that wood siding is at least 6 inches off the ground at all points. Are there gaps between boards or panels? Are the corners tightly joined? Check plywood

Figure 11

An example of a poorly maintained wooden exterior in need of scraping, primer, and painting.

panels for any signs of delaminating or rotting at the edges.

Aluminum, vinyl. Aluminum or vinyl siding should not show any cracks, deterioration, or missing nails (Fig. 12). These sidings should be flashed at the roofline to prevent water from entering. All seams between siding and door or window frames should be caulked thoroughly. Caulking compound should still be supple; any caulking that is cracked or crumbling needs to be replaced.

Fireplaces

Houses built since 1950 have fireplaces and chimneys constructed under modern building codes that specify proper firebrick and mortar. These modern fireplaces also have steel members that help hold the fireplace together during an earthquake. Fireplaces built prior to 1950 may not be as structurally sound.

To inspect a fireplace, start at the exterior and look for cracks or loose mortar. This is an indication that the bricks are loose and could fall in a violent windstorm or earthquake. The only solution is to rebuild or brace the chimney back to the roof. For this you will need to consult with a masonry contractor. Chimneys for fireplaces or fireplace stoves should extend at least 2 feet above any roof section or wall that is within 10 feet of the chimney. (See also "Chimneys" later in this chapter.)

Most residential fireplaces are for small ornamental fires, one big log or two or three small logs. (If you like to burn paper or cardboard in your fireplace, keep the fire small.) It is very important that the fireplace have a spark arrester. This is simply a device that holds a quarter-inch mesh screen over the chimney to prevent sparks from

Figure 12

Asbestos shingles.

starting a roof fire. If a fireplace is not drawing properly and smoke is coming into the house, possible remedies include extending the chimney, adding a draft-enhancing chimney top, or pruning trees near the house. A chimney sweep or fireplace supply company may be able to provide advice.

If you have any questions about the integrity of your fireplace, have it checked by a masonry contractor.

Masonry Fireplaces

In older houses masonry (brick) is the most common type of fireplace and chimney.

The fireplace consists of the hearth, the firebox and damper, and the chimney.

If the firebox opening (the area that opens into the house) is over 6 square feet in area, the hearth should extend at least 20 inches in front of the opening and at least 12 inches on either side of the opening. Check the firebox lining (usually a gray brick) for excessive cracking in the bricks or the mortar. Loose mortar needs to be removed and regrouted. Broken firebricks can be easily replaced by a brick mason.

The damper is the metal flapper in the throat of the fireplace that can be closed when the fireplace is not in use. Check to see that the damper is not corroded and that it operates freely.

The chimney may be unlined or brick-lined with terra cotta (red clay) or other materials. Of concern are interior or exterior cracks and any settlement of the chimney foundation that has produced a separation between the house and chimney.

Wood mantels should be at least 12 inches from the top of the firebox opening.

If there is any question about the integrity of the fireplace or chimney a chimney sweep should be contacted to make a thorough inspection and cleaning.

Factory-Built Fireplaces

Factory-built fireplaces (sometimes called zero-clearance fireplaces) consist of a metal firebox, sometimes lined with firebrick or other refractory (heat-resistant) material, a built-in damper and a factory-built chimney, usually with a stainless steel inner liner.

It is not uncommon for these fireplaces to be provided with glass doors, a fan, and outside combustion air. The doors, the combustion air, and the damper control the rate of wood burning and provide a comparatively efficient heating system.

The hearth and mantel requirements for factory-built fireplaces are the same as those for masonry fireplaces except that hearths for factory-built fireplaces may be installed directly on wood floors. Factory-built chimneys should not be swept with conventional chimney sweep brushes, as these will scar the lining and may lead to failure of the chimney. Specific chemical salts may be used to clean the chimney while a fire is burning.

High-efficiency fireplaces with glass doors or outside combustion air need to have their chimneys cleaned more frequently than masonry fireplaces. The greater efficiency means that more heat is kept from going up the chimney, but so are the smoke and the creosote produced by the burning wood.

Fireplace Stoves

Fireplace stoves (free-standing or Franklin stoves) come in a wide range of designs. There are, however, a few general rules.

Clearance of less than 18 inches from a stovepipe (the singlewall chimney running from the stove to the ceiling) to the wall may indicate that the unit was not installed properly. However, if wall shields of tile, brick, or brick-lined panels are present, less than 18 inches of clearance between the stove and the wall may be acceptable. In order to function properly and not transmit heat directly back to the wall, these shields must be spaced at least 1 inch from the wall, which allows air to circulate between the wall shield and the wall. Brick or tile applied directly to the wall provides little or no protection since the radiant heat from the stove is conducted through the shield to the wall.

If you can determine who manufactured the stove, the local building inspection department, the manufacturer, or a local distributor can tell you the required clearance and hearth requirements.

Heat shields are metal panels mounted inside or outside the stove but attached to the stove, allowing an air space to separate them. If the stove lacks heat shields the clearance from combustible (wood-framed) walls should be at least 36 inches, unless the manufacturer's specifications indicate otherwise.

Gas Log Lighters

A gas log lighter is usually just a capped piece of pipe with many small holes drilled along the top. The valve to operate the lighter must be outside the fireplace opening, but within the same room and within 4 feet of the fireplace opening.

Gas logs should be installed only in fireplaces that have either no damper at all or a damper altered such that there will be an opening up the chimney at all times. This prevents waste gases from inadvertently coming back into the house.

Windows

Whether the windows are aluminum or wood-frame, inspect both the exterior and interior for weather protection. Both types should have flashing and counterflashing to prevent rain and cold from entering (Fig. 13). Check the interior of stationary windows below the sills to determine if the wood is damp or brittle to the touch. If so, water is probably seeping in from outside and damaging the wood.

Are the windows the double-hung type? If so, check the glazing material around the window glass. This material should not be brittle, cracked, or missing. Are the wood frames in need of repair or replacement? Note if the windows are of single-pane or dual-pane (thermal) construction. Windows closer than 18 inches to the floor and those next to a door should be tempered or safety glass.

Be sure to test all movable windows. They should open and close easily, align properly, and stay open as required. Note any broken sash cords or hardware.

Figure 13

Left: *Properly flashed window, as seen from the inside.*

Right: *Exterior of a finished window.*

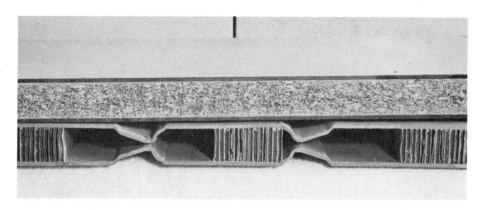

Figure 14

A solid-core door placed on top of a hollow-core door.

Exterior Doors

Exterior doors should be solid-core, and at least 1-3/8 inches thick (for security—not required in most places). Knock on the door to see if it's solid or hollow—you can hear the difference (Fig. 14).

Open and close each door—they should operate smoothly. If a door sticks badly, especially in dry weather, take a second look at the house structure to see if there's a larger problem.

To be properly weather-protected, the door should have weatherstripping around the jambs or door edges. The jambs should be in good condition. Be sure the threshold below the door is secured to the floor and flush to the door.

Door Security

Some jurisdictions require that a front door be a solid-core door at least 1-3/8 inches thick with no glass or recess panels. A solid-core door (with security locks of 1-inch throw or deadbolt) and a viewer is standard.

A decorative door with lead glass or frail plastic is not a good security risk. Any kind of glazed, glass, or plastic paneling on either side of the door can easily and quietly be broken by securing the glass to an adhesive-type holder. A glass cutter or sharp instrument can be used to puncture the area either in the door or nearby so that someone could easily reach in, unlatch the door, and gain entry into the home without disturbing anyone. The most common type of burglary is where a channel-lock plier or a large pipe wrench is used to break off the door knob. A nonsecurity door is therefore both unsafe and could be cause for a higher insurance premium.

Keep these kinds of security concerns in mind during your inspection of the front door area, the back door area, the ground floor windows and glass, and the setback from the street. Observe bushes, trees, fences, and anything else that could obstruct the view of people passing on the street or could muffle the sound of someone breaking in.

Figure 15

Deadbolt. A 1-inch thrust throw is the minimum length required.

Figure 16

Attic access in closet ceiling of master bedroom.

Figure 17

Attic access in hallway ceiling.

Roof and Ceiling Framing

Before you examine the roof close up, take a quick look from the street. From each side of the house, inspect the roofline in relation to the walls and horizon. Is the ridge straight or humpbacked (sagging in the middle)?

Unless you're inspecting a flat roof, look for an attic access opening in a hallway ceiling or closet, or in the garage (Figs. 16 and 17). The opening should be at least 22 by 30 inches, with a tight-fitting cover. If the access is in the garage, its door should be a minimum of 5/8 inch sheetrock and should have a self-closing device.

Working from the attic or crawl space, first check the rafters. (*Note*: Don't step in the spaces between the ceiling joints.) Typical rafter and joist spans are shown in Figure

18. Measure rafter spans from the outside wall to the ridge in a flat (horizontal) plane. The allowable span varies with the roof's *slope*—the vertical rise in inches for each 12 inches of horizontal run. (For example, a roof that rises 4 inches for every 12 of run is called a 4 in 12 roof.) You may also find purlins (2″ × 4″s or 2″ × 6″s placed across the rafters) and braces, designed to reduce the rafter span. (A bearing wall is a main support.) (Fig. 19). The braces must be resting on a bearing wall. In this case, measure the span from the outside wall to the purlin, then from the purlin to the ridge.

While the appearance of sagging in the rafters may trouble you, rafters can display a fair amount of sag (1-1/3 inches over 20 feet) and still be within code guidelines. However, one or several random out-of-whack rafters may indicate a structural problem. If a tile roof has been added since the house was built, the rafters may be sagging from the added weight.

Figure 18

Rafter and joist table for no. 2 or better Douglas Fir

	MAXIMUM ALLOWABLE SPANS				
SIZE	SPACING CENTER TO CENTER	FLOOR JOISTS	CEILING JOISTS	ROOF RAFTERS*	
				LESS THAN 4/12	GREATER THAN 4/12
2 × 4	12″		12′8″	11′0″	11′0″
	16″		11′6″	9′10″	10′1″
	24″		9′10″	8′3″	8′3″
2 × 6	12″	10′11″	19′11″	15′11″	17′3″
	16″	9′11″	18′1″	14′2″	15′11″
	24″	8′6″	15′6″	12′4″	13′0″
2 × 8	12″	14′5″	26′2″	20′11″	22′9″
	16″	13′1″	23′10″	18′9″	20′11″
	24″	11′3″	20′5″	16′3″	17′11″
2 × 10	12″	18′5″	33′5″	26′8″	29′1″
	16″	16′9″	30′5″	23′11″	26′8″
	24″	14′4″	26′0″	20′8″	21′10″
2 × 12	12″	22′5″		32′6″	32′0″
	16″	20′4″		29′1″	28′6″
	24″	17′5″		25′2″	23′3″
LIVE LOADS—FLOOR 40 # Sq. Ft. ROOF 20 # Sq. Ft.					

The span tables for roof rafters are for standard roof loads (composition or wood shingles) and do not include partition loads. In areas subject to snow loads, the weight of snow will reduce the allowable spans considerably. The weight of snow is determined by local building departments based on wind exposure, wetness of snow, and intensity of snowfall. Contact the local building authorities for this information.

Ceiling joists are typically 2″ × 4″s or 2″ × 6″s, and they usually aren't a problem. If these are sagging significantly, you'll see it in the ceiling downstairs. If the attic has been remodeled recently for living or storage, larger joists should have been added—they're now "floor joists" as well.

Trusses, either manufactured or job-built, are common in modern tract homes. A truss combines rafter and ceiling joist in one assembly, allowing much longer spans with smaller-dimension lumber. Be sure no part of any truss has been cut or damaged.

A purlin is a structural member, usually 2″ × 4″ or 2″ × 6″, running perpendicular to the rafters and braced down to a bearing wall. It is used to increase the allowable span for a rafter.

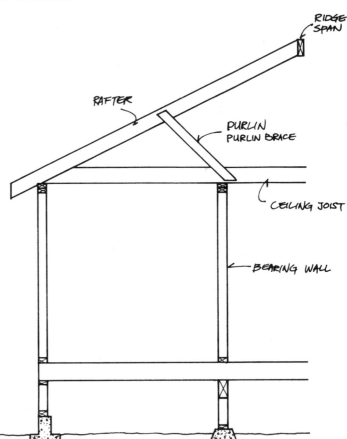

Figure 19

Rafters, braces and purlins.

Attic Area

While you're in the attic, take a moment to check the attic vents. There should be about 2 square inches of vent opening for every square foot of attic. Vents may be in the gable end walls, under the eaves, or up through the roof (Figs. 20 and 21). Proper vents are either corrosion-resistant material with quarter inch mesh openings or fixed louvers.

Figure 20

Attic vent in a home under construction.

Attic vents serve to eliminate moisture build-up, dry out moisture or dampness in the foundation, and provide ventilation that inhibits dry rot and deterioration of wood.

From the attic access, you can also see if there is ceiling insulation. Insulation is measured in R values, an expression of the resistance of the material to the transmission of heat. The higher the R value, the more heat is retained in cold weather. As a rule 5-1/2 inches of insulation gives you an R value of 19; 9-1/2 inches of insulation provides about R-30.

If the insulation has a layer of foil facing, the facing material must be in direct contact with the ceiling or some other thermal barrier. The facing on regular household insulation is highly flammable and must not be exposed. (For details, see the section "Insulation" later in this chapter.)

If there's an attic ventilation fan, be sure it's working properly and that the noise isn't deafening. Check for signs of leaks and for proper flashing around the perimeter.

Finally, take the time to inspect the rafters, roof sheathing, and ceiling for water stains that would signal a leaking roof.

Figure 21

Attic gable end vent after construction has been completed.

Roofing Materials

Roofing materials range from clay tile (which is very heavy) to aluminum or foam (which are very light). New roofing methods are being approved all the time. If you see something unusual or unfamiliar, ask the local building department or a local roofing contractor about proper installation standards.

Figure 22

Composition shingle roof in good condition (note "eyebrow" type attic vent).

Figure 23

A well maintained wood shake roof.

When inspecting a roof, keep safety firmly in mind. Whenever possible, work from a secure perch like a well-anchored ladder or an upstairs window. Try to avoid walking on the roof. In addition to examining the roofing material, be sure to look at the flashings—the metal pieces used in the gutters and wherever the roof ties into a vertical surface (a chimney or roof jack) or the plumbing vents pass through the roof. Minor rusting is OK, but if you see a lot of rust you should anticipate problems soon.

The expected lifespan of a roofing system depends on a number of factors: the quality of the materials, the roof-

er's skill in installation, local climate (wind, sun, rain, snow, ice, fog), and the roof's slope.

The most popular roofing materials are composition shingles, wood shingles, wood shakes, tar and gravel, and tile. Here's how to evaluate each type.

Composition shingles, asphalt or fiberglass, come in many colors and are easy to maintain. There can be as many as three layers of composition shingling on a roof at one time; the average lifespan is 15 to 25 years in moderate climates. The minimum allowable pitch is 2 in 12—otherwise the roof will leak.

Composition shingles consist of protective mineral granules. When the shingles shed these granules, a residue will be evident at the base of the downspouts or in the gutters. If shingles are cracked, blistered, curled, or simply missing, the roof is suspect. Wiggle some shingles—if they are brittle and break easily, the roof needs to be replaced (Fig. 22).

Wood shingles have a smooth, uniform texture; *wood shakes* are rougher and thicker at the bottom (Fig. 21).

Life expectancy is about 15 to 25 years in moderate climates. To replace a wood shake roof, the entire roof must be removed, repapered, and then reshaked. Wood shingle and shake roofs fail when they become so dried out and shrunken that the nails no longer hold or the wood splits where the nails were driven.

Some communities prohibit wood roofs or require that they be treated with fire-retardant chemicals or fireproofing. If the house is in a hilly, heavily wooded, or bushy area, ask the local fire or building department about restrictions on wood roofs.

Tar-and-gravel built-up roofs are usually found on newer homes that have flat or very low-pitched roofs. Several layers of asphalt-saturated felts are glued together with hot asphalt (tar) and surfaced with gravel or rocks (Fig. 22). The most important thing to find out is whether the roof was surfaced by a licensed roofer. The average life-span of these roofs depends on the quality of the work, and no more than two tar-and-gravel roofs are permitted by code. (To determine the number, count the gravel stops at the roof edge.)

Built-up roofs are prone to leakage and need more or less continual repair. Look for evidence of ponding, water sitting in the low points on the roof. If there is ponding the roof will be more subject to leakage in that area, and the weight of the water may cause more sagging.

These roofs should pitch to a proper drain or gutter; excessive water settling or ponding in any area must be corrected or it will lead to leaks. If you want to test the drainage, turn a garden hose on up top and see where the water goes (Fig. 24). If there is excessive ponding the roof-

Figure 24

Tar-and-gravel roof. Water settlement (ponding) is due to poor drainage.

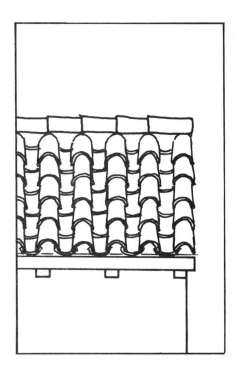

Figure 25

A tile roof.

ing material should be removed and a new rigid insulation board (celotex, for instance) should be installed to provide a slope.

Tile roofs may be clay or concrete (Fig. 25). Since the roof must be able to structurally support the weight, tiles average 9 pounds apiece, rafters must be larger, and solid plywood sheathing is required for seismic bracing. A slope of 3 in 12 is the minimum for a tile roof.

Advantages of a tile roof are:
- Good for the lifetime of the home, barring severe freezing and thawing.
- Will not burn.
- Lower insurance rate.
- Rich looking and beautiful.
- Works on a pitched roof (minimum slope 3 in 12).

Disadvantages of a tile roof:
- Weight is 900 pounds per 100 square feet of tile.
- Roof rafters have to be larger.
- Roof must have solid sheathing of half-inch exterior plywood.
- Works best on simple gable roof.
- Cost is high.
- Tile roofs should not be walked on.

Figure 26

Check skylight for proper flashing and sealant around perimeter and for evidence of water seepage in the interior ceiling.

Skylights

Today there are a large number of skylight models on the market. While it used to be common for skylights to be mounted on curbs extending at least 4 inches above the roof, new building codes allow self-flashing skylights to be shingled right into the roof with only the dome protruding (Fig. 26). The popular double-dome design helps discourage condensation and provides some insulating value. Openable skylights double as warm-air vents in summer. Older glass and wire-glass skylights are more troublesome, often requiring yearly maintenance. Dried-out sealant must be replaced, and weepholes (small openings in the downhill side of the frame that permit drainage) must be cleaned and kept open.

Whenever you see a skylight, find out the name of the contractor who installed it, then ask if it's guaranteed. From the roof, check carefully for proper flashing and sealant. From inside, study the underside of the roof or the interior ceiling for any evidence of water seepage.

Chimneys

The exterior of a chimney should be in good condition and properly weather-protected. Is it straight, or is it pulling away from the roof or exterior wall? Proper flashing is required where the roof and chimney connect (Fig. 27).

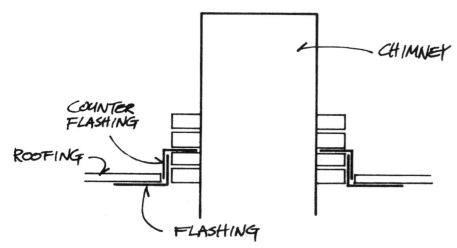

Figure 27
Chimney flashing.

Look for the spark arrester (Fig. 28). A spark arrester is a device constructed of nonflammable material, 12-gauge minimum welded or woven wire mesh, with 1/2-inch openings, or cast iron plate of 3/16-inch minimum thickness or other satisfactory material. State codes require that the spark arrester on the chimney be visible from the ground.

A chimney cap or bonnet prevents wind and rain from entering the chimney. Caps should be securely attached and not rusted through.

Locate the area where the ashes are deposited—this may be outside or inside the building. A metal coverplate should be securely flush to the wall.

(For details on fireplaces, prefabricated fireplaces, and woodstoves, see "Fireplaces" earlier in this chapter.)

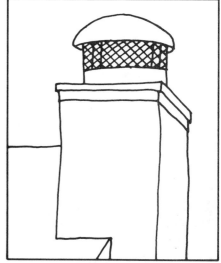

Figure 28
An example of a spark arrester (perforated cast-iron plate) with a 12-gauge wire mesh screen (left) and a chimney cap or bonnet (above).

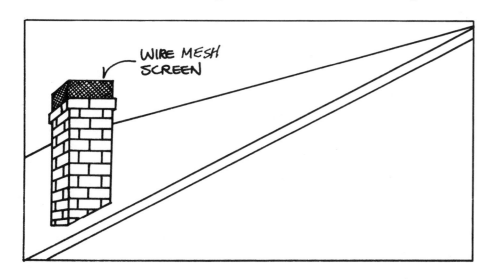

Gutters and Downspouts

Gutters and downspouts are made of galvanized steel, aluminum, plastic, or redwood. Check for rust if they're steel, dry rot if redwood, or cracking if plastic. Plastic gutters are somewhat easier to work with initially, but in extremely hot climates they may dry out, crack, or lose their shape. Are there missing sections?

Gutters should be parallel to the edge of the roof and slope slightly toward the downspouts. Are they anchored securely? Downspouts should be firmly joined to gutters and braced to exterior walls with downspout brackets (Fig. 29).

Do gutters and downspouts leak? Are they plugged up? Place a water hose on top of the gutter, turn it on, and let the water run (Fig. 30). Check the outflow from the downspouts: Is water channeled away from the house or does it pool up?

Standing water may accumulate and cause foundation problems or excess moisture in the crawl space or basement. In most cities, downspouts cannot be connected to sewer lines or drain across another property unless that is the direction of natural flow.

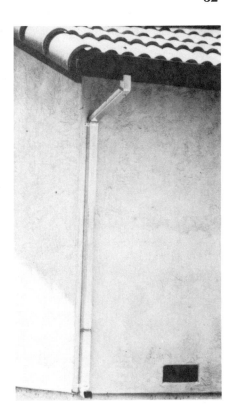

Figure 29

Downspout is securely connected to gutter and wall with brackets. In most cities, downspouts may not be connected to sewer lines. Check where roof water drains. Water from one property cannot drain across another property unless it is part of the overall natural flow.

Figure 30

A gutter with an unobstructed opening to downspout. Gutter is properly secured to roof edge.

Insulation

Home insulating materials are measured in terms of their R value—the higher the R value, the less heat transmitted by the material. Ideally, exterior walls should be insulated with materials rated at least R-11; floors and attics need at least R-19, though R-30 is the current standard for attics of new homes.

There are four basic types of insulation: fiberglass, rockwool, cellulose, and foam.

Fiberglass is the most common insulating material in the western United States. Made of noncombustible spun glass, it is most often sold in batts (blankets), though fiberglass can also be blown or poured into walls.

Fiberglass has an R value of about 3.4 per inch of thickness. So batts 5-1/2 inches thick are needed for areas requiring an R-19 rating, and a thickness of 9-1/2 inches will reach R-30 (Fig. 31). Although some compaction will occur over time, fiberglass retains its insulating qualities.

Rockwool is processed from rock or slag. Generally gray in color, rockwool is usually installed as loose fill in the attic. Though similar to fiberglass in noncombustibility and R value, rockwool loses its insulating qualities over time as it settles and compacts considerably.

Cellulose insulation is made of milled paper that has been treated with fire-retardant chemical salts. Its R value is about 3.7 per inch of thickness, but compaction over time will reduce its effectiveness. Also, some building codes prohibit the use of cellulose fill in attics or walls that have

Figure 31

Check insulation for adequate R values: R-11 in walls, R-19 in floors and ceilings (R-30 in ceilings of newer homes).

electrical wiring running through them. To preserve air space around the electrical wiring, some contractors install wire nets that keep the insulation in place.

Foam insulation   has a value of about 6.25 per inch of thickness, but most foam is extremely flammable. Because foam may also release gaseous chemicals, most building codes prohibit the installation of foam in an area directly exposed to the atmosphere.

Fiberglass or other mineral fiber insulation may have a facing glued to blankets of the insulation. The facing makes it easier to install the insulation blankets, and it provides a moisture barrier so that condensation in the insulation will not work through to the building finishes. The facing may be kraftpaper (tan or gray) or foil with a kraftpaper backing. In either case, the asphalt cement used to glue the paper or foil to the fiberglass blanket may produce a highly flammable gas when exposed to heat. For this reason, in an attic, the facing must be in direct contact with the ceiling below. In walls, the facing must be in contact with the plywood or sheetrock surface; in floors, the facing must be in contact with the subfloor.

Because heat rises, most of the radiated heat loss (loss other than from opening doors and windows and through cracks and vents in the building) from a house is up through the roof. Attic insulation having a value of R-19 is almost always cost-effective, and insulation of R-30 or R-32 may be worthwhile in very cold climates or in homes that have less-efficient, expensive electric heat.

Most of the rest of the radiated heat loss is through the walls. Insulation with an R-11 value (usually 3-1/2 inches of fiberglass) is cost-effective. However, retrofitting an uninsulated house by pumping insulation into the walls through drilled holes may not be cost-effective; ask the local utility company for information on the amortization period for such an installation.

Since heat does travel up, very little heat is lost through the floor assembly, and retrofitting the floor with insulation will not be cost-effective in most cases.

Double-glazed windows, which have two panes of glass with an air space in between, reduce the heat loss through the window by about 60 percent. But since windows are a relatively small area of heat loss in most houses, double-glazed windows are of questionable economic value on new construction. (For more information on energy efficiency, see "Energy Efficiency" in Chapter 5.)

For newer homes, a certificate of insulation may be on file with the local building department (Fig. 32).

THIS IS TO CERTIFY THAT INSULATION HAS BEEN INSTALLED IN CONFORMANCE WITH THE CURRENT ENERGY REGULATIONS, CALIFORNIA ADMINISTRATIVE CODE, TITLE 25, STATE OF CALIFORNIA, IN THE BUILDING LOCATED AT:

_____
    Street   Lot Number   Tract Number

EXTERIOR WALLS

    Manufacturer_____Thickness/Type_____R Value_____

CEILINGS

Batts: Manufacturer_____Thickness_____R Value_____
Blown: Manufacturer_____Thickness_____No. Bags_____
                                                 Wt./Bag_____
              Sq. Ft. Covered_____R Value_____

FLOORS

    Manufacturer_____Thickness/Type_____R Value_____

SLAB ON GRADE

    Manufacturer_____Thickness/Type_____R Value_____
              Width of Insulation_____Inches

FOUNDATION WALLS

    Manufacturer_____Thickness/Type_____R Value_____

GENERAL CONTRACTOR_____LICENSE NUMBER_____

By_____TITLE_____DATE_____

INSULATION CONTRACTOR_____LICENSE NUMBER_____

By_____TITLE_____DATE_____

Figure 32

For homes built in California since 1977, state regulations require the builder and the insulation applicator to sign a card certifying that the proper R values for all insulation locations have been installed. This certificate is filed with the local building department in the jurisdiction of the property address.

Interior Walls and Ceilings

Check the interior walls and ceilings of all rooms for holes and cracks. If all the interior walls are covered with either vinyl wallpaper or wood paneling, you might be justified in suspecting that these coverings are hiding excessive and continuous cracking of the wall finish. Sometimes cracking is due to the normal up-and-down movement of a house built on adobe soil, but cracking may also be an indicator of a serious structural problem.

Spray-applied acoustical ceiling readily shows water stains, which may indicate a roof or plumbing leak. Also look at areas around the heating louvers. Discoloration here may indicate a leaking heat exchanger (a potentially dangerous situation) or may just show that the heating ducts need cleaning. Contact the local gas utility and ask if they will inspect the furnace.

Be sure to check bathroom and kitchen walls and ceilings for mildew and dry rot from steam and other moisture.

Asbestos

If the house was built between 1945 and the early 1970s, there is a chance that asbestos was applied to the ceilings. (Asbestos was also used for house siding and to insulate furnace ducts, flue pipes, and gas heaters and boilers.)

If the asbestos remains intact and is fully enclosed by ceiling or wall finishes, it often poses no problem. But airborne asbestos poses considerable health risks. Its microscopic daggerlike fibers lodge in the lungs and other internal organs, causing asbestosis (an irreversible scarring of the lungs), and cancers of the lungs, stomach, large intestine, rectum, and other organs.

If you suspect that the house contains asbestos insulation or asbestos tiles, do not disturb the material. Contact the nearest federal or state office of the Occupational Safety and Health Administration (OSHA). They will send a certified specialist to take air samples and perform follow-up laboratory tests. Asbestos removal can be quite expensive and must be performed by a technician trained and certified by the Environmental Protection Agency (EPA).

Interior Floors

Are the floors in the building hardwood? Are they in good condition? If possible, lift up the carpeting to inspect the floor below. When walking, do you feel some unevenness? If the wood is buckling, water may have settled on the floor and caused damage.

Look especially closely at floors in the kitchen and bathrooms: sink, shower, and bathtub areas are all prime spots for dry rot. Is linoleum or ceramic tile in these areas in good shape? If linoleum is the covering, are there baseboards or top-set rubber baseboards or equivalent wood at least 4 inches high? If you suspect dry rot, contact a competent contractor or structural pest control company.

Stairways—(Interior *and* Exterior)

Walk up and down the stairway. Does anything feel amiss? The minimum tread depth (run) is 9 inches, and the maximum rise (height) is 8 inches. The largest tread depth or riser height in any flight of stairs should not exceed the smallest by more than 3/8 inch (Fig. 33). If nonslip material is peeling off the steps, it must be replaced. Private stairways must be at least 36 inches wide, and any stairway with four or more risers should have a

Figure 33

An uneven step in a stairway, such as illustrated here, is a potential safety hazard.

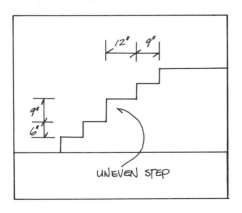

UNEVEN STEP

Figure 34

Note absence of handrails. If stair has four or more steps, a handrail should be provided. Railings along the edge of the porch should not have openings larger than 6 inches in diameter.

handrail (Fig. 34). Handrails should be placed between 30 and 34 inches above the nosing of the stair tread. All open stairways, balconies, and landings over 30 inches from the ground must also have intermediate railings or other barriers so that a sphere 6 inches in diameter cannot pass through (Fig. 35).

Do you have to duck walking up or down? The stairway should have a vertical clearance of at least 6-1/2 feet at all points, measured from the tread nosing to the soffit (the underside of the overhanging arch) above. The depth of the landing should be no more than 7-1/2 inches below floor level. A door at the top of a stairway should not swing out over the top step except for screen doors.

Figure 35

This stairway railing is in violation of safety standards: The railing has an opening in excess of 6 inches in diameter.

Porches and Decks

Wood decks and porches are likely spots for earth-wood contact; be sure to inspect the underpinnings carefully (Fig. 36). The deck framing is also a good jumping-off point for termites bound for the main house. Check for metal flashing between deck and house, or at least air space between the two.

Decks and porches more than 30 inches above the ground must be protected on the open sides by guardrails at least 36 inches high.

Decks or balconies above the first floor must be designed to support more weight than the interior floor system, as large groups of people may occasionally congregate there. If in doubt, be sure to have a structural engineer take a look.

Fiberglass roofing panels for patio roofs should overlap securely and should not be cracked. If they're not securely nailed to the support beams or rafters, they'll rattle—or even blow off—in a strong wind.

Is the patio roof adequately braced to the existing house structure? Beams and rafters holding the fiberglass panels should be secured to the ground and house, and they should be evenly spaced to carry the load. Are supporting beams vertical from the roof to the ground?

Figure 36

Patio decks should be supported by concrete piers that are anchored in the ground. Wooden posts should not come in contact with the soil.

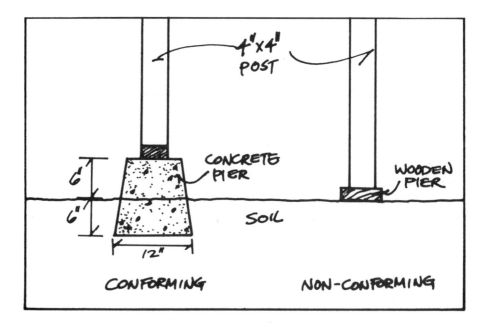

Garage

Inspect the garage's structure using the same methods as for the main house. The garage floor should be noncombustible material. A fire separation wall is required

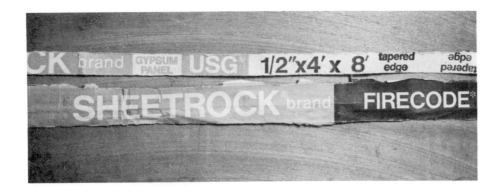

Figure 37

A one-hour fire resistant material is required between the garage wall and the living area. Sheetrock must have the proper firecode label. The label here does not meet current standards: 5/8-inch sheetrock is now required.

between living areas and an attached garage. This wall must be a minimum of 2″ × 4″ wood studs, spaced 16 inches on center, and covered with 5/8-inch type-X sheetrock on the garage side of the wall (Fig. 37).

If there's a door from the garage to the main house, it must be a solid-core door 1-3/8 inches or thicker with an approved self-closing device. Check the garage door: It should operate smoothly and fit flush to the ground so that water can't back up onto the garage floor.

Note any garage vents—they prevent the buildup of car exhaust. One opening of 60 square inches per car stall is recommended (Fig. 38). All air ducts in the garage must be of 26-gauge steel for fire protection; factory-made, flexible air ducts are not permitted to pass through the firewall into the living area.

A garage should not be used for living quarters unless it has been approved as habitable by the building department.

Figure 38

Garage vents are recommended, but not required.

Drainage

Drainage around the exterior perimeter of a building prevents water from backing up into the foundation and interior of the building.

Accessory Buildings

Accessory buildings should not be a public nuisance and must be safe for the use intended. Make sure the entire structure is within the property line. Some jurisdictions also require minimum setbacks from the property line. Accessory buildings at the rear and side require one-hour fire-rated construction materials with no openings if any wall is within 3 feet of the property line.

An accessory building should not be used as a dwelling unit. If the building is attached to the main house, you may wish to have the building department inspect it for code compliance.

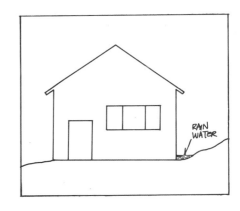

Figure 39

Example of poor drainage on the right side of building. Drainage of surface water to eliminate ponding of water near foundation should run away from the foundation as illustrated on the left side of building.

Structural Concerns for Residential Buildings in Earthquake Country

Most people think of an earthquake as a terrifying, devastating event, complete with panic-stricken people running in the streets, fires out of control, and buildings toppling from their foundations.

Earthquakes are dangerous occurrences, but since the 1933 earthquake of Long Beach, California, earthquake (seismic) resistant buildings have been designed, and (as the professionals are learning), it is possible to design buildings which can withstand all but the most violent of earthquakes.

During an earthquake, older homes can be shifted off their foundations by the movement of the earth. The walls can lift up and hit the ground with such force that windows, window frames, and doors crack and the floor become uneven. Old building codes in the California Bay Area prior to World War II did not always require that sill plates be bolted to the foundations or that pony walls (installed between the foundation and floor joists) be cross or diagonally braced with plywood sheeting.

Buildings meeting the Uniform Building Code's seismic requirements (commonly enforced in most of the United States) are generally earthquake-resistant, but not earthquake-proof. They should not collapse in a major earthquake, but might sustain some expensive damage.

Homes built prior to 1952 may not be bolted to the foundation. Before the code requirements instituted in 1952, it was common to drive nails partially into the bottom of the wooden mudsill (large horizontal members forming the bottom frame of the house) and set this mudsill into the wet concrete. An earthquake of relatively mild force could force the building to shift off its foundation. Check to see if the structure has a raised floor; you may be able to see nuts and washers through foundation vents, or at the garage mudsills. Fix the structure with expansion bolts inserted into the drilled holes in the foundation, steel expansion straps bolted to the foundation, the side of the wall, and nailed to the mudsill, studs, or floor joists.

Older homes with high first floors may have unbraced pony walls. This design was very common in the late 19th and 20th centuries. Typically there are many steps up from the sidewalk to the porch. If unbraced, pony walls will almost certainly fall in minor earthquakes. A quake-damaged building with these walls may be salvaged by being moved back into position, and jacked up to put in a new wall. The expense is obviously great, as are the chances of major contents damage, and fire loss due to broken gas and electric lines. The simplest way to brace standing pony walls is to add 1/2″ thick plywood to the interior (crawl space) side of the studs that make up the pony wall.

But what can you, the home buyer or owner, do to safeguard your most expensive purchase and protect your family?

After deciding which area you would like to live, ask your realtor to show you homes not in a special studies zone for earthquakes. Don't buy a house in a fault zone. After purchasing your home, have either a general contractor, a professional engineer, or an architect inspect the structure and advise you on what further construction is needed to prepare the house to withstand an earthquake. (It may help you to know that all homes built in California since 1952 have followed the Uniform Building Code, and are strengthened to withstand all but the strongest of earthquakes.)

What would the contractor or engineer be looking for? They would first determine if the foundation was adequate for the size and height of the structure. The soil would be analyzed to see whether it is capable of supporting the foundation. Then they would check if the mudsill (the 2″ × 4″ or 2″ × 6″ wood between the concrete and framing) is properly bolted to the foundation. They would also check for adequate shear wall bracing (the frame of the structure tied together so the structure can withstand heavy winds and earthquakes).

Foundation

Two common types of residential foundations are the concrete slab and the raised or perimeter foundation. The concrete slab became popular in the 1950s, especially among subdivisions. The majority of these homes used anchor bolts to secure the framing to the concrete slab. The raised or perimeter foundation is one where the house sits on top of a continuous foundation that extends around the entire building. These houses sit above the ground, 18″ from subfloor to the soil under the house (18″ to floor joists or 12″ to girder), depending on whether the house is built on a hillside. The space between the ground and the wood floor is called the crawl space.

The short walls between the floor and the foundation are called cripple walls. Older and modern homes may have inadequately braced foundation cripple walls, and may collapse in an earthquake. To reduce the chance of these walls collapsing, they are required to be properly sheathed. Anchor bolts installed between four and six feet apart and one foot away from the ends of the sill plates will help lessen the possibility of the walls collapsing.

Some common construction failures are caused by homes built with raised foundations which sit between 18″ from subfloor to the soil under the house and have no sheathing or diagonal bracing to support the wood studs in position. When an earthquake occurs, sometimes a house built on this kind of foundation will rotate and fall off the foundation.

Walls

Interior and exterior woodframe walls that lack solid sheathing are prone to severe damage during a quake. Installing plywood to unsheathed walls will reduce physical (and financial) loss in the event of an earthquake. Masonry walls without steel reinforcement may develop cracks or collapse. Cracks larger than 1/8 inch are a serious concern and a licensed contractor should be contacted to evaluate the problem.

Chimney

Nail plywood or add metal straps to tie chimney onto the ceiling joists, reducing the danger of falling masonry. Prior to 1967, chimneys were usually built of unreinforced masonry; the materials used in holding the brick together may be deteriorating, resulting in loose bricks.

Roofs

Secure all roof tiles (slate, terra cotta, etc.) from falling off with nails or tie wires.

Additions

Additions of second stories above a garage, with narrow unsheathed panels on both sides of the garage walls, may collapse in an earthquake. Improperly anchored home additions will separate from the original structure if bolted down incorrectly. Contact a licensed contractor to inspect and evaluate the need for additional bracing, and check the mudsill to see if it is properly secured to the foundation.

Exterior Stairs, Wood Decks, and Porches

Inspect the exterior wood members for deterioration, rotten wood, or termites. Strengthen the footings, supports, and lateral bracing by installing metal connectors. Strengthen all structures that are attached to the house.

Gas Appliances

Install flexible gas connectors where gas lines join appliances. Existing copper gas connectors are not flexible and should be inspected for possible leaks after a quake.

Water Heater

Install galvanized plumber's tape around the water heater tank and attach to wood studs (2″ × 4″) on each side of the tank with 1/4 inch diameter lag screws or bolts. A typical water heater weighs about 450 pounds when filled. When a water heater falls over, the movement will break the gas and water line connectors.

Air Conditioners on Roof Areas

Add support bracing for air conditioners installed on the roof area.

Trees and Shrubbery

Remove all tall or large tree branches that may fall on top of your house.

Site

Is your home on stable soil or rock, a hillside near a fault area, adjacent to utility lines or towers, near a retaining wall, or buildings that are taller than your home? Be sure you are familiar with the type of ground your home is built on. A house built on bedrock is more stable than one built on unstable landfill soil.

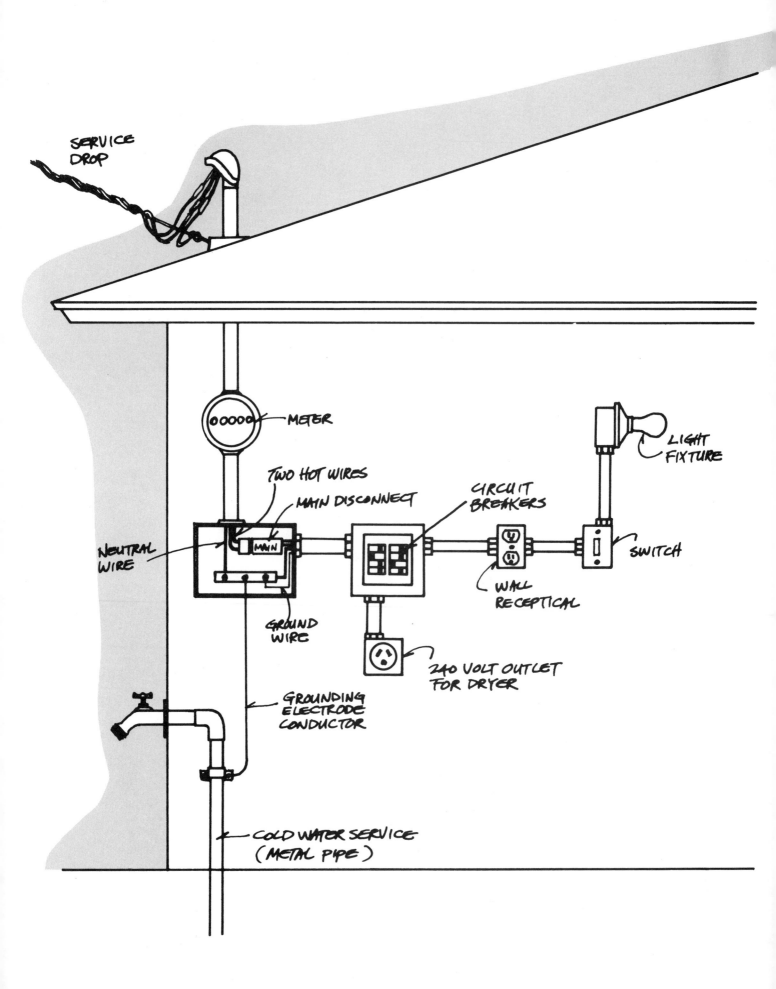

SERVICE DROP

METER

LIGHT FIXTURE

TWO HOT WIRES

MAIN DISCONNECT

CIRCUIT BREAKERS

NEUTRAL WIRE

MAIN

SWITCH

WALL RECEPTICAL

GROUND WIRE

240 VOLT OUTLET FOR DRYER

GROUNDING ELECTRODE CONDUCTOR

COLD WATER SERVICE (METAL PIPE)

The Electrical System

Utility companies usually provide power at 240 volts to the house system. The overhead cable outside the house from the utility pole is called the service drop. The service drop wires are connected to service entrance conductors that terminate in a meter or meter-main box (Fig. 40).

Depending on the type of installation, the wiring is divided either at the meter-main or at a subpanel by connecting into three busses, assemblies that collect and distribute the current. The voltage is divided by having two hot-leg busses and one neutral (or grounded) bus. If 240 (or 220) volts are needed, as for an electric oven, the power for the appliance is taken from both hot legs; if 120 volts are needed, as for a light, the power is taken from one of the hot legs and the neutral. (The hot-leg wires and neutral wires are insulated; the electrode conductor is uninsulated. This only applies to the service entrance conductors. The neutral is *always* insulated on the house side of the service entrance.) The grounding electrode conductor is bare and connected to a ground rod, to steel in the foundation, or to the water piping.

Fuses or circuit breakers are inserted between the busses and the wiring to appliances and outlets. If 240 volts are needed, two fuses are installed; if a single circuit breaker is used, it will cover two busses (called a two-pole breaker). If two breakers are used on a 240 volt circuit, they must be joined by a coupler, so they function together.

National Electric Code

The purpose of the National Electric Code is to protect people and property from hazardous uses of electricity. Changes are made to the Code every three years so it is

Figure 40

Opposite: *Overview of residential electrical system.*

45

advisable to always check with local inspectors. It is dangerous when inexperienced persons install wiring. They may not be aware that they are overloading a wiring system or making an improper connection, or they may not know how to handle the materials properly in conformity with the National Electric Code. For the sake of safety, it is therefore wise to hire only licensed electrical contractors whose workers have completed a rigid training program. As long as your electrician gets a permit and has his work inspected by the proper authority, you are protected. Your inspector will check everything on the job to make sure it is done properly.

Evaluating the Service Rating

At the main panel there may be just the electrical meter and a main breaker or main fuses (usually 100 amperes but may range from 60 amperes to 225 amperes) or the meter and the breakers or fuses for all the circuits in the house. If the main panel has only the main breakers or fuses, one or more subpanels will be found in the garage or house.

Residential services range from two-wire, 30-amp panels up to three-wire, 225-amp panels. To evaluate a home's service rating, look at the main panel (or the meter and main disconnect on the exterior of the house or garage). If there's overhead service in the area, just follow the wires down from the power pole and weatherhead.

The service rating in amps may be printed on the label inside the panel's cover. If not, check the individual breakers or fuses—up to six—that comprise the disconnect. You will find one of the following situations:

1. The smallest size (usually found on homes over forty years old) is a 30-amp, two-wire service. You will see two wires dropping from the power pole to the meter and main disconnect. The main disconnect will have only one or two plug fuses. This type of service is capable of producing only 2,880 watts—or one lighting circuit and one appliance circuit. You'll probably find only one electrical receptacle in each room. Two-wire services cannot run appliances that require 220 volts: electric clothes dryers, air conditioners, or ovens.

2. The next size up is a 30-amp, three-wire panel providing both 120 and 240 volts and about 5,520 watts (Fig. 41). This service also provides one lighting circuit and one appliance circuit that could operate an electric clothes dryer but little else. Many older homes are still getting by with this service.

Figure 41

Thirty-ampere service. Note location of main switch shut-off handle above four-circuit fuse panel.

Figure 42

Sixty-ampere service. Main and range combination. Four-circuit fuse panel shut-off handles for main service and range are located above circuit fuses.

3. A 60-amp, three-panel, which was common in the 1940s (Fig. 42). This panel consists of a 60-amp pull-out main disconnect and a 60-amp pull-out switch for the range. The range pull-out typically has one 25-amp fuse for the range and four plug fuses for lighting and appliance circuits. This combination switch sometimes feeds a small subpanel inside the house.

4. A 100-amp, three-wire service will accommodate the average modern household of 1,500 to 3,000 square feet, with garbage disposal, dishwasher, clothes dryer, a couple of appliance circuits, trash compactor, television, etc. It is considered the minimum service for new or remodeled houses by the National Electrical Code for single-family dwellings.

If the house has electric heat or cooling, a 125, 150, 200, or even 225-amp service may be appropriate. However, there is some leeway since no household ever uses all the appliances at the same time. An electrical inspector or an independent contractor can help you calculate the necessary service rating.

How easy or costly is it to upgrade service and wiring that's inadequate? It depends in part on the type of house construction.

Main Service Panel and Subpanels

The main service can be mounted directly on the exterior if it is a weatherproof type that has a top lip to prevent rain from entering the box. An indoor type may also be mounted outside if it is enclosed in a weatherproof shelter (Fig. 43).

In many residences, especially older houses, the main panel contains all the circuit breakers or fuses for the house. However, it's increasingly common to place the meter and a main disconnect on the exterior, and then locate a subpanel that houses the breakers or fuses in the garage, utility room, or interior hallway (Fig. 44). For a time, subpanels were often located in clothes closets, but current codes prohibit this because of the fire hazard. Panels in crawl spaces or other accessible areas are also usually illegal. Even if the main panel houses fuses or breakers, a subpanel houses fuses or breakers, a subpanel or two may be found in the house, making it easier to wire circuits.

Check to see that the main service panel is not rusted. Does the door open and shut easily? Is the door weather-protected? For safety reasons, the main disconnect should not be placed higher than 7 feet from the ground nor less than 30 inches above the ground. There should be

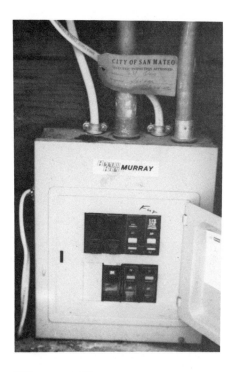

Figure 43

Each circuit breaker should be labeled. Also shows illegal romex installation on top left of box.

Figure 44

Each circuit breaker should identify what function it controls. All unused openings are sealed off.

no openings in the panel; any unused openings should be sealed off.

If there are fuses, check them (Fig. 45). In older homes you'll find Edison base or plug fuses, which screw in like lightbulbs. These fuses pose a problem: Someone could inadvertently substitute a 30-amp fuse for a blown 15-amp fuse and not realize the danger. The overload could generate excess heat and cause a fire. To eliminate this problem, type S fuses were invented. All that's necessary is to install a nonremovable adapter for a 15-amp or 20-amp fuse that will reject a fuse of a larger size. Once installed the adapter cannot be removed.

Take the plate off the inside of the panel to get a look at the wiring. Is it in good shape, or is there a surplus of electrical tape, frayed connections, or rust and discoloration due to heat or oxidation? The panel should show no double-lugging—two circuits running off the lug designed for one. Double-lugging is a fire hazard.

Figure 45

Main service panel, 60-amp, 220-volt service.
1. *Adapter for nontamperable S type fuse.*
2. *Nontamperable S type fuse.*
3. *Edison base fuse.*
4. *Main pull switch for entire service.*

Similarly, burned-out fuses in the panel or any evidence of smoldering or fire may mean the electrical service is overloaded, and you may need to install a service with a higher rating.

Wiring Methods and Materials

The most common wiring method used for residences during the last forty years is nonmetallic sheathed cable (usually called romex or NM). This system has two or more insulated wires and one bare groundwire inside a plastic or fabric-covered sheath. Splices in NM wire may be done only inside a junction, outlet, or fixture box, and these boxes must be accessible. The splices may be made with cone-shaped plastic devices (wire nuts), mechanically crimped metal tubes or simply soldered together and taped in the box.

Older houses are usually wired with a knob-and-tube system (Fig. 46). Conductors in this system are separated by air space. The knobs are insulators that hold the wiring away from wood framing. The tubes are ceramic pieces that isolate the wiring from wood wherever the wiring passes through bored holes. Flexible woven tubes called looms were used where there was little clearance between conductors. Splices in a knob-and-tube system are made by wrapping the wires around each other, soldering, and taping the finished joints. There is nothing inherently wrong with the knob-and-tube system as long as it hasn't been compromised by later additions. In the attic check for a mix of nonmetallic cable and knob-and-tube. If NM cable has been spliced in the open, you may wish to inspect the system.

It is common in older houses to see 220-volt conductors, if there are any, in a metal conduit (Fig. 47).

Grounded outlets should be installed in the kitchen, bathrooms, and laundry room. Recent codes are requiring ground fault protection on bathroom, kitchen, and garage receptacles. If the house system is not grounded, individual ground wires to the water piping system may be installed.

Figure 46

Old knob-and-tube wiring. This is an excellent system if not disturbed.

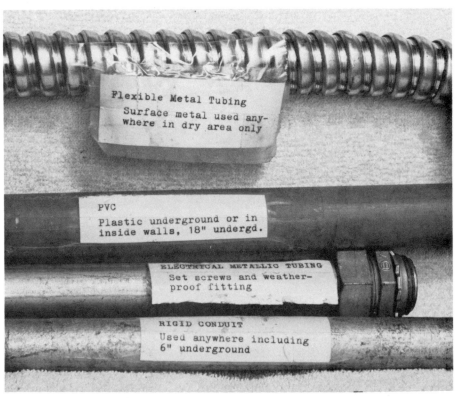

Figure 47

Some types of protective electrical tubing.

As a general rule, there is no real need to have grounding receptacle throughout a house.

Typical household appliances and outlets have the following electrical requirements:

	AMPERAGE	VOLTAGE	WIRE SIZE
Electric dryer	30 amps	220 volts	#8 aluminum or #10 copper
Electric oven-range	50 amps	220 volts	#6 aluminum or #8 copper
Air conditioner	30 amps	220 volts	#8 aluminum or #10 copper
Kitchen outlets	20 amps	110 volts	#10 aluminum or #12 copper
Family room, dining room outlets	20 amps	110 volts	#10 aluminum or #12 copper
Lights	15 amps	110 volts	#12 aluminum or #14 copper
Other outlets	15 amps	110 volts	#12 aluminum or #12 copper

There are many exceptions and variations to these general requirements. For example, if the oven and range are wired separately, each may have a 30-amp circuit. Older houses may have all 15-amp or all 20-amp light and outlet circuits.

The circuit size is determined by the load served, and the fuses or circuit breakers are designed to protect the wire size used. A 15-amp breaker or fuse, for instance, is intended to prevent a #14 copper wire (the smallest wiring allowed for permanent wiring) from overheating and possibly burning. Note that the lower the amperage, the larger the wire size. The difference in sizes for aluminum and copper wiring reflects the fact that copper is a better conductor.

If you can take the face plate off the panel board where most of the circuit breakers or fuses are located, you should be able to see the conductors. Most likely, the largest ones will be silver-stranded cables and the others will be copper-colored single wires (Fig. 48). But if the house is less than thirty years old and all the wires, including the small 15- and 20-amp wires, are silver-colored, you can assume the entire house was wired in aluminum.

Aluminum wiring installed in homes between 1965 and 1973 is less stiff and less stable than copper. Over time aluminum wiring tends to become loose or to oxidize and create heat buildup, especially at connection points such as switches and receptacle outlets. If the house has aluminum wiring, check for the following danger signs:

- switches or outlets that become hot to the touch, smoke, or spark

- the smell of burning plastic or burning insulation around switches or outlets

- flickering of all appliances on an outlet or an entire circuit

If the house is completely wired in aluminum, have an electrical contractor examine the system and tighten connections. In the worst case, outlets and switches may have to be replaced with devices designed for use with aluminum wiring.

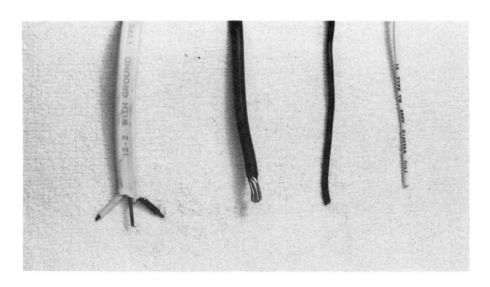

Figure 48

Left to right: *Romex wire with ground wire; multistranded aluminum wire; #12 wire used for 20-ampere fuses; #14 wire used for 15-ampere fuses.*

If the house is wired with romex, you can determine the wire size by reading the markings on the outer sheath. If there are no markings on the sheath or the insulation that covers the individual wires, it is difficult to establish the actual size and amperage of the wiring. If everything looks okay and it appears that the original wiring hasn't been tampered with, assume that the wire going into a 20-amp breaker is #12 copper and wire going into a 15-amp breaker is #14 copper. Copper wiring #10 is usually a single strand; larger sizes are multistranded.

Zip Cord

The most hazardous misuse of residential electrical systems is wiring with zip cord, a light-gauge wiring similar to extension cord. Zip cord may be as small as #18 gauge—two full sizes smaller than the #14 copper wire that the smallest house circuit is designed to protect from overheating.

ANY ZIP CORD WIRING SHOULD BE IMMEDIATELY REMOVED.

GFI or GFCI

Standard circuit breakers or fuses serve only to protect the wiring from overheating, not to protect people from being electrocuted. The only device for preventing electrocution is the *ground-fault circuit interrupter (GFI or GFCI)* (Fig. 49). The GFI senses the current flow between the hot and neutral conductor in a circuit. Whenever there is a deviation of at least 5 milliamps, the sensor will interrupt the current flow. Since the human heart begins to fibrillate (beat rapidly and irregularly) at about 5 milliamps, the likelihood of electrocution is eliminated.

GFIs may be located on the main panel or in a special outlet (usually in or near the bathroom, kitchen, or garage) and can be identified by small buttons that read Test and Reset. The GFI should be tested periodically to make sure it is functioning.

Receptacles and Switches

Check each room to make sure there are at least two electrical receptacles, or one receptacle and one light fixture. The kitchen should have at least two receptacles that are on separate circuits.

For safety, the receptacles should be the U-slotted or grounded type (Fig. 50). In a newer building wired with nonmetallic sheathed cable, a separate grounding wire runs from the U-shaped slot all the way back to the panel. If a short circuit develops in any electrical device, the current will go through the grounding system and open the

Figure 49

Ground-fault circuit interrupter (GFI), located on a bathroom wall.

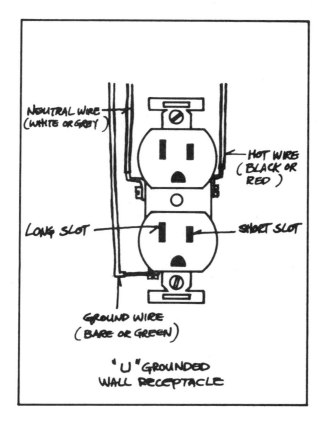

NEUTRAL WIRE
(WHITE OR GREY)

HOT WIRE
(BLACK OR
RED)

LONG SLOT

SHORT SLOT

GROUND WIRE
(BARE OR GREEN)

"U" GROUNDED
WALL RECEPTACLE

Figure 50

U-grounded wall receptacle.

circuit breaker or fuse to interrupt the circuit. Receptacles
in bathrooms, kitchens, laundries, and outdoor areas
should be grounded.

Check all coverplates on light switches and wall receptacles. Broken or cracked plates, receptacles, and
switches need to be replaced. Test all switches and receptacles. To check a receptacle, plug in a night light or a
simple circuit analyzer.

Pull-Chain Fixtures

Old-style pull-chain fixtures consist of a lightbulb, a
porcelain socket, and a chain. One simply pulls the chain
to turn the light on or off. Though once popular, these fixtures are hazardous because the socket can crack or break
and make contact with the metal casing. The fixture and
the chain then become energized and can shock or electro-
cute the user. Some pull-chain fixtures have insulating
links that provide some protection. However, it's best not to
have pull-chain fixtures at all. Plan to replace them with
standard fixtures and wall switches.

Electric Ranges and Cooktops

Run some tests to be sure the electric range—or separate oven and cooktop—work properly. Turn the burners
on and make sure the heating elements turn red. See if
the oven works.

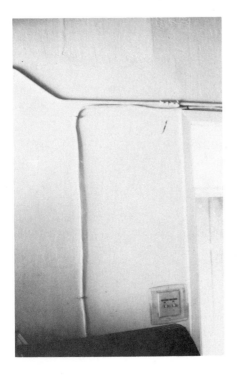

Figure 51

Romex wiring in a garage. Horizontal wiring is properly enclosed in metal tubing, but the vertical running wire has no protective covering. All romex wire should be concealed within the walls or be installed in metallic tubing where less than 8 feet from the ground.

Lift up the burners to be sure the areas underneath are accessible for proper cleaning. Check the wall plug and the receptacle coverplate for damage.

Don't forget to turn off the dials after you're done.

Wiring in Detached Garage or Carport

Wiring in the garage should be concealed within the walls or be installed in metallic tubing where less than 8 feet from the floor. If the garage walls are sheetrock or panel, be sure you are familiar with any electrical wiring installed behind the walls. It's hazardous if nails or sharp objects penetrate the wiring behind the concealed wall.

Light fixtures, outlet coverplates, light switches, and plug outlets should be in good condition. Is there a U-grounded outlet for the clothes washer? The washer and dryer should run off a separate 20-amp circuit. Electric dryers should have their own 30-amp, 240 volt circuit.

Service Drop Clearance

Is the main service drop from the power pole to the house at least 10 feet above the ground and at least 12 feet above the driveway? These clearances are required so that fire engines can drive close to the house in case of fire or emergencies.

Do the wires, weatherhead, and meter appear to be in good shape? If in doubt about the service drop, contact a utility company representative or the local building department.

Figure 52

An example of an unacceptable main service drop. Wires must be at least 10 feet above the ground and 12 feet above the driveway area.

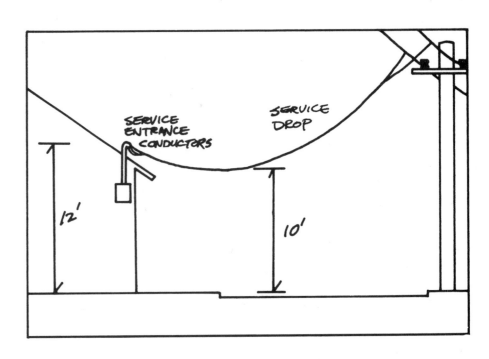

Use this page for your own notes and questions.

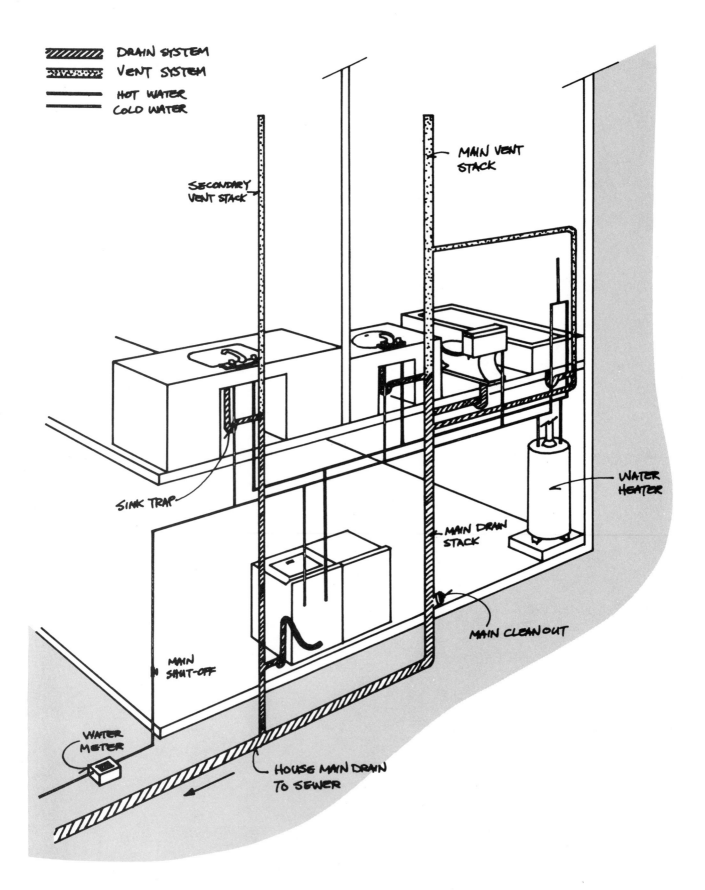

DRAIN SYSTEM

VENT SYSTEM

HOT WATER
COLD WATER

SECONDARY
VENT STACK

MAIN VENT
STACK

SINK TRAP

WATER
HEATER

MAIN DRAIN
STACK

MAIN CLEAN OUT

MAIN
SHUT-OFF

WATER
METER

HOUSE MAIN DRAIN
TO SEWER

The Plumbing System

An overview of a typical residential plumbing system is shown in Figure 53. It includes:

- a supply system
- a domestic waste-vent (DWV) system
- plumbing fixtures (water heater, sprinkler, toilet, shower, bathtub, sink)

In addition, houses in rural areas that have no central sewage system have individual septic tanks and leach fields.

Local plumbing codes detail requirements for all water supply and waste pipes and specify rules for the installation of all plumbing fixtures. Exterior water pipes are usually galvanized, copper, or plastic; interior pipes are either copper or galvanized iron. Since codes vary by jurisdiction, check with your local building department for specifications.

Water Supply System

Water from the serving utility flows through a water meter located either at the property line or, in cold climates, within the house. In some water districts there are no meters and residents pay a flat rate for service.

The main shut-off valve is always mounted above grade and usually located near the front of the house, on the same pipe as the outdoor faucet.

Normal water pressure off the main pipe should fall between 15 and 80 pounds per square inch (psi). Use a water gauge to test the pressure at the hose bibb nearest the main pipe (Fig. 54). If the water pressure exceeds 80 psi, the main pipe should have a pressure regulator (Fig. 55). Excessive pressure can cause faucets to leak and can damage dishwashers and clothes washers.

Figure 53

Opposite: *Overview of water supply and domestic waste-vent (DWV) systems.*

57

Figure 54

Water-pressure gauge connected to outside main hose bibb. Note main shut-off valve at bottom of pipe.

Figure 55

If water pressure exceeds 80 pounds per square inch, a pressure regulator is required.

Typical residential water supply pipes have a 3/4-inch or 1-inch interior diameter. The size of the pipe depends on the available water pressure, distance from the water main, and the number and type of fixtures served. As a rule of thumb, houses with sprinkler systems should have at least 1-inch water service. Branch lines off the main pipe are usually 1/2-inch pipes with flexible 3/8-inch connections to the various valves.

In areas where the water is high in minerals and salts (hard water), part of the residential water supply may be directed through a water softener before it branches off to the water heater and other fixtures. Usually the outside faucets and sprinkler systems receive untreated water. If the water is quite hard, any galvanized iron pipes are likely to suffer internal corrosion that may restrict the water flow to unacceptable levels. Check the flow by running water into the bathtub farthest from the water main. If the flow is very slow, have a plumber evaluate the system.

Domestic Waste-Vent (DWV) System

The waste-water system within the house consists of drains, traps, and vents (Fig. 56). Waste and vent pipes are usually made of plastic (PVC or ABS), cast iron, or galvanized iron. In rare cases, copper tubing is used.

Each plumbing fixture has a drain that is outfitted with a trap, a U-shaped piece of pipe that holds a small amount of water and prevents sewer gases in the drain lines from escaping back into the house. (Sink traps are readily visible under the sink; toilet traps are concealed within the fixture.) Each trap has a vent, a vertical air pipe that extends at least 6 inches above the roof. By

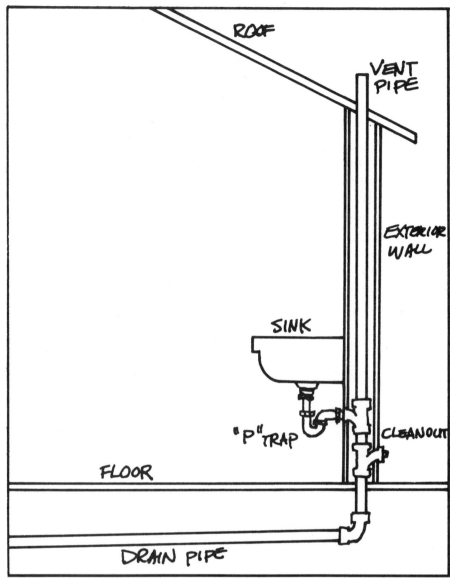

ROOF

VENT
PIPE

EXTERIOR
WALL

SINK

"P" TRAP

CLEANOUT

FLOOR

DRAIN PIPE

Figure 56

Location of vent pipe, drainpipe, and sewer clean-out.

breaking the suction created by the waste waters passing through the trap into the drain, vents prevent the siphoning of the trap.

Water then passes from the trap into the house drain, into the sewer lateral, and finally into the city sewer or private septic tank.

At the uphill termination of all long runs of drain and sewer lines there is a clean-out, a threaded cap that can be removed so that blockage in the pipe can be rodded out. Clean-outs are also present at the foundation line outside the house, toward the street, and at the property line, near the sidewalk.

An improperly installed clean-out has no value. The access to any clean-out or minimum crawl space under floor joists is 18 inches. No clean-out should be located in a space less than 30 inches in width. Clear working space from clean-out to the foundation wall or other obstruction must be at least 18 inches for waste lines exceeding 2 inches in diameter, or 12 inches for a 2 inch diameter and

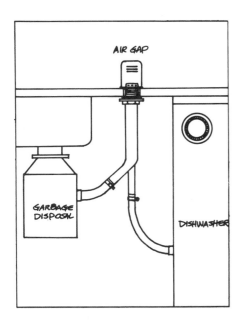

Figure 57

Air gap for garbage disposal unit. Check to be sure opening is not clogged by refuse.

smaller. Clean-outs are required at the base of a stack, the upper end of a horizontal drain or its branches, and at the change or direction specified by the code. The interval of installing clean-outs should not exceed 100 feet measured by the developed run of the pipe. Clean-outs may be required at intervals of 50 feet due to the low scouring potential on line with little slope. The size of the clean-outs must be as large as the line it serves. However, a 4 inch clean-out would normally serve any of the larger lines. No clean-outs shall be installed inside of a sump or interceptor. Access by crawl space opening must be provided within 20 feet of any clean-out under the house, or the clean-out must be extended to the exterior of the house.

Older houses typically have a stack (main vent) that is the same size as the water main. Newer houses may have several vents that serve different fixtures. Standard trap and vent sizes are:

	TRAP	VENT
Toilet	internal	2″
Washbasin	1-1/4″ or 1-1/2″	1-1/2″
Kitchen sink	1-1/2″	1-1/2″
Clothes washer	2″	1-1/2″
Shower	2″	1-1/2″
Bathtub	1-1/2″	1-1/2″
Laundry tub	1-1/2″	1-1/2″

Older houses that have 1-1/2-inch clothes washer standpipes may need to have 2-inch pipes installed if a newer high-volume washer is to be used.

Air Gaps

Air gaps in the plumbing system prevent contaminated water and waste from siphoning into appliances or into the house water system. Air gaps are commonly found in:

- Garbage disposal or kitchen sink trap to dishwasher. The air gap is mounted on the sink drainboard and prevents back-ups in the sink or disposal from flowing back into the dishwasher (Fig. 57).

Figure 58

Sprinkler anti-siphon valve is located at the turn-on for the sprinkler system.

- Hose bibbs or sprinkler systems. Atmosphere relief valves prevent water from the hose or sprinkler system from being siphoned back into the house water system (Fig. 58).
- Anti-siphon ballcocks in toilet tanks.

Water Heater

The cylinder of a typical water heater is approximately 5 feet tall (Fig. 59). At the top of the cylinder, there is a pipe and an on-off valve that controls the supply of cold

Figure 59

Components of a gas water heater.

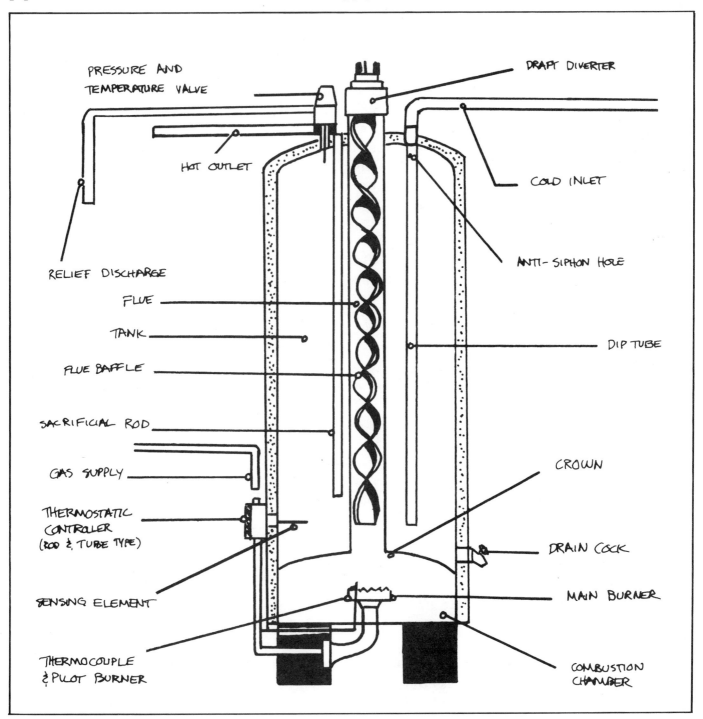

water. Also on the top is the discharge pipe. The interior of the heater consists of a filling tube (or dip tube) that extends down to within 6 inches of the bottom of the heater. The water on top of the heater is hot and the water entering at the bottom is cold. When the dip tube becomes cold, it engages the switch in the thermostat and the burner is turned on. When the water reaches the desired temperature for which the thermostat is set, the burner shuts off.

A gas-fired water heater has a vent or chimney-like portion with an upside-down cone called a draft diverter. The vent allows unburned gases and heated air to pass through the roof. The vent pipe should rise at least 12 inches above the roof.

Below the water heater is a valve for draining the unit. Manufacturers recommend that water heaters be flushed periodically (about every six months) through a hose attached to the valve. Flushing removes accumulated sand, rust, or other sediment. Ask the current owner when this was last done.

The temperature-relief valve is designed to prevent buildup of excess heat and pressure in the event of a malfunction (Fig. 60). A water heater that lacks such a release device can explode and cause a great deal of damage. The temperature relief valve is spring-loaded and is designed to open under pressure. It will allow water to drain from the tank until the pressure returns to normal. Often, though, after a valve has opened under pressure it does not properly reseal and will leak or drip.

A gas-fired water heater should not be installed in a bedroom, bathroom, closet, or any area opening onto a bedroom. If it is located in a garage, it should have seismic bracing and most jurisdictions require that the water heater be elevated so that the flame is 18 inches above the floor, to prevent the heater from igniting gasoline vapors, causing a fire. If a gas water heater is located in an enclosed area, a minimum of 100 square inches of free-air openings must be provided within 12 inches of the top and bottom of the heater (two 10″ × 5″ wire mesh screens are acceptable).

Approved gas connectors are "flex" (teflon or vinyl-coated flexible metallic piping) or aluminum, but *not* copper, which has a tendency to break down and clog the flow of gas. An electric water heater requires a separate switch and circuit breaker feeding it, or it may be tied directly into a junction box if the junction box is controlled by a breaker.

Check the thermostat. Manufacturers warn that using the high-temperature setting shortens the life of a water heater; the higher the temperature setting, the long-

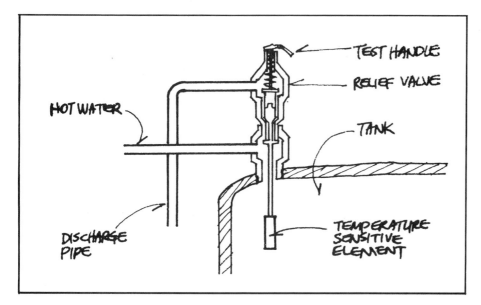

Figure 60

A temperature-relief valve prevents excess buildup of heat and pressure in a water heater.

er the heater must run. Very high water pressure can also damage a water heater.

A rotten-egg odor may be caused by hydrogen sulfide formed by the impurity in certain magnesium anode rods. This condition can usually be corrected by removing the rod and replacing it.

A water heater that has been working for a number of years may develop a rumbling or popping noise. Such noise indicates that the heater is heating the sediments lying at the bottom of the tank. The best thing to do is to drain the heater and flush it with a special cleaning compound.

If the water from the temperature and pressure-relief valve runs continuously, shut off the cold-water supply valve, remove the pressure-relief valve, and replace it.

If you can't ignite the pilot, either the thermocouple or the magnetic portion of the valve that holds it open needs replacing. The thermocouple can easily be changed by the average homeowner, but the magnetic portion must be done by a qualified repairman.

Solar Water Heater

There are two basic types of solar water heating systems found in residences. Both require special inspection by an expert if any malfunction or improper installation is suspected.

Active solar systems   involve flat plates mounted on the roof facing approximately south. Water is pumped through the plates, where it is heated, and then returned to a storage tank or oversized water heater. An active system has an electric pump and temperature-sensing equipment. Although they tend to require more maintenance, active systems are usually much more efficient than passive systems.

Passive solar systems are simply tanks on the roof that collect hot water either directly or from attached panels. No pump is used—the house water pressure simply pushes the water through the system with the help of convection (hot water rises, cold water settles).

The most important point in inspecting a solar water-heating system is to verify that all pipes, valves, knobs, and the like are labeled as to function and that the operating instructions, including emergency procedures, are posted nearby.

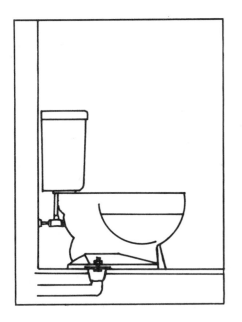

Figure 61

Above: *Toilet bowl should be securely fastened to floor by bolts at base of toilet.*

Figure 62

Right: *The fluidmaster assembly has fewer moving parts than the ballcock assembly.*

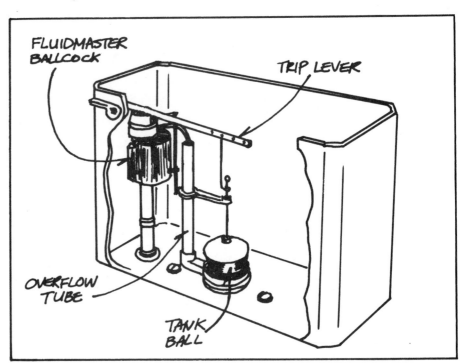

Toilet

First, observe whether the toilet porcelain is cracked or missing at any point of the tank or bowl. Is the toilet secured properly to the bathroom floor or can it be rocked back and forth? There should be at least two bolts holding the toilet to the floor—one on each side of the toilet (Fig. 61). Check for leaks around the base; if you find one, the wax seal will need replacement or other repair may be necessary.

Now lift up the tank top and see if the internal assembly is a ballcock or fluidmaster type. Fluidmaster types are being used more frequently because there are fewer moving parts—no ballcock or floatball valve (Fig. 62). Whatever the type, does it appear to be in good repair?

Flush the toilet and let it fill. Then if it keeps running, the tank ball may be worn out such that it no longer makes a positive seal to shut off the water or the water level may be set too high, allowing excess water to drain continuously down the overflow standpipe. Either replace the tank ball or adjust the tank so that it shuts off before it reaches the top of the overflow.

Showers and Bathtubs

A house may have a combination tub-shower, a shower enclosure, or a standard bathtub. If the shower or tub-shower has a glass door, tempered safety glass, or approved plastic is required. Check the mark identifying it as such, typically at the bottom corner of the door. A cracked door could pose a serious hazard and should be replaced.

The shower head, faucets, and spout should all be in good working condition. Turn them on and check to see that they don't leak. Are the flanges (escutcheons) for the shower head and faucets secured to the wall?

Does the grouting and sealing around the tub-shower or bathtub need repair? Are there any damages or cracks or missing grout on the tub or shower walls? Any leakage can cause rotting in the wood framing and floor. If you notice damage, the area should be inspected by a structural termite company. Repairs can be expensive.

Bathroom Sink

Is the washbasin in good condition? Are there cracks, missing pieces of porcelain, or other defects? If mounted in a vanity cabinet, check the inside for signs of leaking and rot. If simply mounted to the wall or free-standing, check that the sink is secured tightly.

Turn the faucets on, then off. Do they leak? It may just be a matter of a washer or two, or something more serious. Check the pop-up stopper—these are notorious for malfunctioning. Be sure there are shut-off valves below the sink; do they turn easily? Also check the trap below the sink; does it leak, show signs of rotting, or is it sealed with tape?

Septic Systems

A residential septic system consists of a septic tank with one or more leach lines. The septic tank collects all the waste materials from the plumbing fixtures and separates the solids from the liquids; solids are then decomposed by bacteriological action (Fig. 63). The liquid effluent passes into a leach line, a gravel-filled underground trench that carries the effluent away from the house and to a

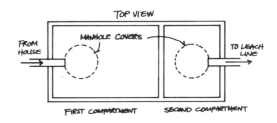

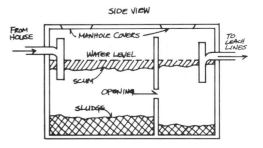

Figure 63

Top and side views of a septic tank. Typical capacity is 1,000 to 1,500 gallons.

How it works: *Each system has two components. First is the septic tank with a liquid capacity of 1,000 to 1,500 gallons. This tank collects waste materials from the plumbing fixtures and separates solids from liquids. The second component is the leach line which disposes of the liquids. The septic tank has two compartments, the first being larger than the second. Solids are decomposed by bacteriological action, the sludge settling to the bottom, and the scum moving to the top. The liquid or effluent in the middle flows to the second compartment where further separation of solids from the liquid is accomplished to have an effluent free of solids.*

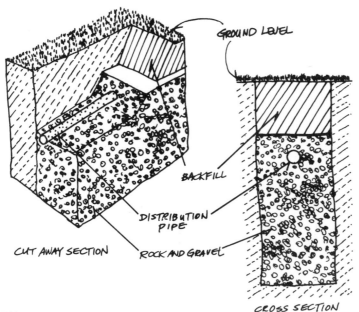

CUT AWAY SECTION

GROUND LEVEL

BACKFILL

DISTRIBUTION PIPE

ROCK AND GRAVEL

CROSS SECTION

Figure 64

The leach line: *A leach line is a gravel-filled subsurface trench of variable depth with the ability to allow liquids to move through the trench and seep into the soil as it passes. The effluent leaches through the trench into surrounding soils at rates determined by the soil structure. For example, clay soils will absorb liquids at a much slower rate than gravelly soil. The ability of the leach line to absorb the effluent changes with years of service as the soil becomes more saturated. Clogging of clay soils can occur more rapidly than gravelly soils. Solids in the effluent will lessen the efficiency of leach lines and failures may occur more frequently, such as surfacing of septic tank effluent.*

Figure 65

A: *If there is more than one leach line, a diversion valve may be found in some systems between the septic tank and the beginning of the leach lines. The diversion valve allows the homeowner the option of directing septic tank effluent flow into one of the two lines. While one leach line is being used, the other will "rest." Rest means drying out of the trench side wall, and the soil-clogging slime and bacterial mat die off. Also, soil particles can return to its normal state from the expansion that occurs when it is constantly wet with the effluent. A good management practice is to alternate leach line use yearly.*

B: *Typical layout of a septic tank and diversion valve separating two lines of a drainfield.*

C: *Two methods for repairing or expanding your existing drainfield. The best insurance against the need for major repairs is a scheduled program of inspection and pumping coupled with the observance of use which may include removal of roots, especial-*

ly where leach lines are near trees, or other obstructions in the sewage line from the house to the tank, clearing of clogged inlets into the septic tank, repair of drainage to lines caused by excavation or ground settling, or clogging a distribution box. In some of the older systems involving wooden tanks, it may be necessary to replace some of the redwood boards which will decay over time.

Major repair normally involves drainfield extension or relocation, most likely as a result of improper maintenance. Where feasible, extension of the leach lines is probably the most economical means of increasing capacity. If relocated, a diversion valve should be considered so that the old and new sections of the drainfield may be alternated.

A

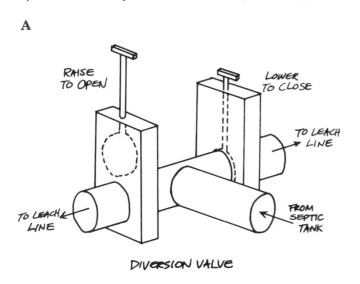

RAISE TO OPEN

LOWER TO CLOSE

TO LEACH LINE

TO LEACH LINE

FROM SEPTIC TANK

DIVERSION VALVE

B

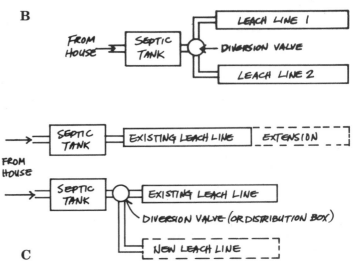

FROM HOUSE — SEPTIC TANK — LEACH LINE 1 — DIVERSION VALVE — LEACH LINE 2

FROM HOUSE — SEPTIC TANK — EXISTING LEACH LINE — EXTENSION

SEPTIC TANK — EXISTING LEACH LINE — DIVERSION VALVE (OR DISTRIBUTION BOX) — NEW LEACH LINE

C

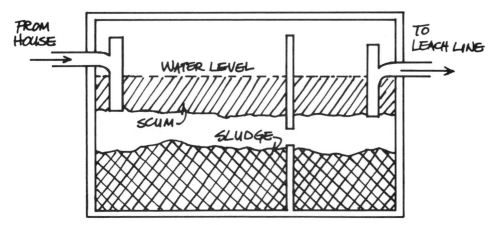

Figure 66

Sludge builds up from the bottom of the septic tank, while scum collects at the top. If the tank is not regularly pumped, the sludge and scum will eventually clog the opening between the two compartments or pass into the second compartment.

drainfield (Fig. 64). If there is more than one leach line, a diversion valve allows the homeowner to direct the effluent to a specific line and allow the other to dry out (Fig. 65).

The location of the septic tank and leach lines are noted in the house's building plans. If these are not available, contact the original builder or architect, or the local health department.

Septic systems require periodic pumping and repair. Sludge and scum should be pumped from the tank every three years (Fig. 66). And nothing must be allowed to obstruct the sewage line from the house to the tank. Similarly, tree roots growing near the leach lines must be removed. Excavation and ground settling may also require minor repairs to the septic system. Older systems that have wooden tanks may occasionally need to have decayed boards replaced.

Two indicators of serious problems with a septic system are: sluggish or inoperative plumbing drainage; surface moisture that has a sewage odor in the vicinity of the leach lines. These problems may require the extension or relocation of the leach lines and the installation of a diversion valve.

Most jurisdictions require that property owners obtain a permit before undertaking any major repair work or new construction on a septic system. On request, the local health department may send out an inspector to check out the system and make recommendations for maintenance and repairs.

To maintain quality service from your septic tank system, repair defects at an early stage and keep up with necessary pumping. Abuse of a system is a cause of early failures. Such abuse includes the excessive grinding of non-biodegradable material in the garbage disposal unit, addition of grease, and the excessive use of strong detergents. One must remember that for a septic system to operate as designated, it must not inhibit natural biological action. Introducing excessive water or unnatural materials can cause failure or a slowdown of bacterial action. The non-use of garbage disposal units will reduce the amount of solids and liquids that go into the septic tank. One simple rule of thumb is to limit materials that are not easily digested by the septic system.

The failure of a septic tank system is indicated by either sluggish or inoperative plumbing drainage, and/or surfacing moisture, with the bacteriological characteristics of sewage and odors in the vicinity of the leach line area. Remember that the sludge is building up and the scum is building downward. When it reaches the opening between the two compartments, the solids will build up in the second compartment. Therefore, proper maintenance is of prime concern in achieving an acceptable service life from septic tank installations. Particular importance should be placed on the periodic removal of sludge and scum by pumping. For optimal performance, septic tanks need to be pumped at three year intervals. This will prevent the build up of sludge and scum, which may get into the leaching system and rapidly clog the lines, leading to septic system failure. IT IS RECOMMENDED THAT ANY PUMPING (WORK OR ADVICE) BE PROVIDED FROM A LICENSED TANK CONTRACTOR.

Use this page for your own notes and questions.

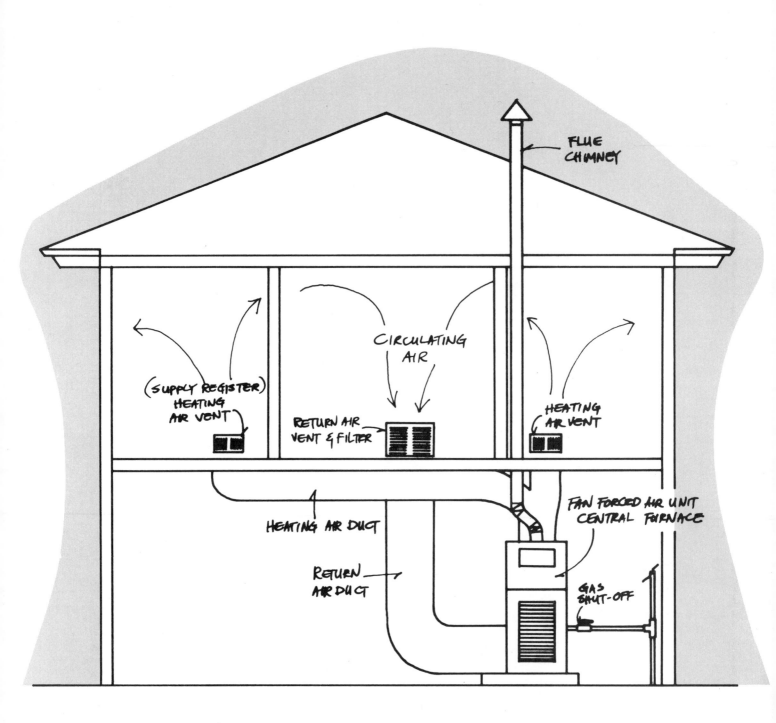

5

Mechanical Systems

esidential mechanical systems are those that heat
or cool the air, and humidify, dehumidify, or purify
the air. Your inspection should focus on the heating
system, exhaust fans and vents, and any roof-mounted
evaporative cooler. (Inspection of the air conditioning system requires a professional.) In addition, you will want to
evaluate how energy efficient the house is.

Begin with the heating system. The following guidelines discuss natural gas or oil, electric, and solid-fuel systems. Solar heating systems are best left to an expert.

Gas or Oil Heating System

A typical gas heating system consists of a main supply connection, furnace, air ducts, floor or wall air vents,
thermostat, and chimney vent pipe, or flue (Fig. 67).

Far rarer are radiant gas heating systems, in which a
gas-fired boiler substitutes for the furnace, and the piping
carries the heated water through a concrete floor slab or to
wall-mounted radiators.

Gas Supply System

The main gas line from the service utility to the
house is 3/4-inch or 1-inch pipe; branches off the main line
are usually 1/2-inch pipe with flexible connectors. The gas
in the street main is under high pressure. A regulator
near the meter reduces the pressure before the gas enters
the house system.

Outdoor gas lines are all wrapped black iron, plastic
coated, or plastic pipe. Older homes may have black enam-
eled pipe. Gas lines should not be installed under concrete
slabs within the house. If there is no underfloor crawl
space, the gas lines must be run through the attic and

Figure 67

Opposite: *Typical gas heating
system.*

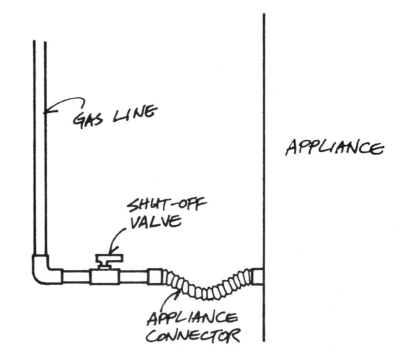

Figure 68

Every gas-fired appliance must have its own shut-off valve located within 3 feet of the appliance.

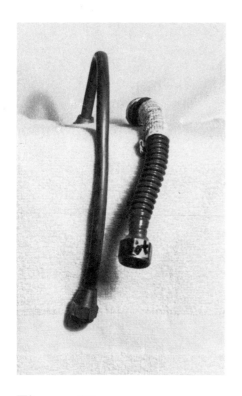

Figure 69

Copper connector (left) is no longer approved for use as a gas connector. *Flexible teflon-coated connector (right)* is one of several approved gas connectors.

then down to the appliances to be served. If there is neither a crawl space nor an attic, gas pipes may run exposed on the roof and around the exterior walls of the building. Gas lines that run across a roof must be raised high enough above the roof that they do not sit in puddles during heavy rainstorms.

The shut-off valve for the gas line is usually located near the meter. This valve requires a wrench to open or shut. In addition, individual gas-fired appliances must have a shut-off valve within 3 feet of the appliance (Fig. 68).

Appliances are connected to the main gas supply by either rigid gas lines or flexible connectors (Fig. 69). Copper connectors are no longer approved for this use, although some brass-copper alloys are allowed. All interior gas lines should be properly secured—not loose or wobbly—and should show no signs of rust or other damage. If you have any questions about their condition, ask the local gas company or a contractor to inspect the lines.

Gas Furnace

A forced-air furnace has a fan that forces the heated air through ducts. The cover of the fan must always be securely in place—a missing cover could cause carbon monoxide to build up. The fan compartment should be clean so that dust and dirt are not recirculated through the house. The furnace should burn with a clean blue flame. A yellow glow or a smoky flame indicates that repairs are overdue.

Gravity furnaces do not have fans; simple convection causes the hot air to rise into the living areas (Fig. 70).

In order to function properly, a furnace must have an adequate supply of fresh air (combustion air). An insufficient air supply will impede complete combustion and may cause the formation of hazardous carbon monoxide. Combustion air is also necessary to provide the draft up the chimney. If the furnace is in a large room, the ambient air supply will suffice. If the furnace is in a small room or clos-

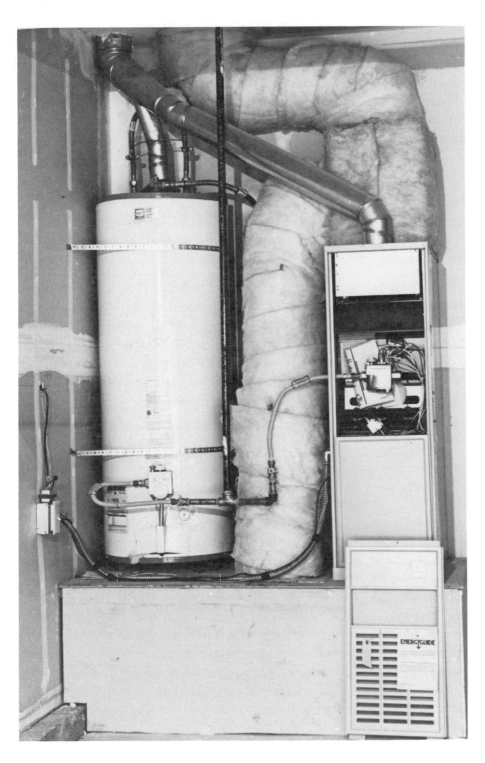

Figure 70

Water heater and upflow (forced air) furnace. Water heater is stabilized by metal straps.

Bonding wires for electrical continuity of ground

Note: *Flexible pipe from temperature and pressure relief valve does not comply with plumbing codes. Piping must be smooth hard-drawn copper or galvanized steel.*

Seismic bracing

Shut-off valves at flexible gas line connection from main line

Furnace electrical disconnect

Platform to provide minimum of 18" above floor (in garage only) et, it should have air openings to the outdoors, the crawl space, or the attic. Combustion air openings should be cleaned and kept free of obstructions.

If the furnace is located in a closet or utility room, there should be at least 6 inches of clearance between the front of the furnace and the enclosure door. Furnace enclosures may not open onto bedrooms or bathrooms. The enclosure should have a switched light.

Most modern furnaces have several safety devices: a temperature-limiting switch that shuts off the furnace if the temperature gets too high; a fuse or circuit breaker that shuts off the furnace in the event of electrical problems; and a microswitch that shuts off the furnace when the fan cover is removed. Testing of these devices can be done only by a qualified mechanical inspector. Many newer furnaces also have electric lighters instead of continuous-burning gas pilot lights.

Floor furnaces are found in older homes. They usually have one large floor grille. The grille should never be blocked by floor coverings or furniture, nor should hallway or closet doors swing open over the grille. If properly serviced, these "antiques" can provide adequate heat for a room.

Wall furnaces are common in additions and parts of houses that are not served by the central heating system. The vents are usually concealed in a wall and cannot be easily inspected. Their surfaces should be free of lint, dust, and grime. Furniture should not be placed in front of a wall furnace, nor should a door open out in front of one.

Ducting and Chimney

All ducts should be tightly fitted. Remove one or two floor grilles and check the ducts for excessive dirt. Flexible air ducts may be used in the house, but only sheetmetal ducts may be used in the garage area. Insulated garage ducts will provide increased heating efficiency.

All gas-fired appliances must have chimneys that remove the combustion gases from the interior of the house. The chimney must run continuously uphill and terminate above the level of the roof. The chimney should be inspected for rust holes, uncovered openings, and other signs of damage. Most single-wall vents (such as those serving the furnace or a gas water heater) should be at least 18 inches away from wood or other combustible materials. Double-vent walls may run within an inch of combustibles. Required clearances are usually marked on the vent or appliances.

Thermostats and Filters

Some heaters have simple on-off valves or switches, but more commonly the unit will be run off a thermostat. The thermostat should be mounted securely on a wall that is well away from the heat source or duct outlet (Fig. 71). Dual-setback thermostats have a timer that allows the homeowner to set the thermostat for different temperatures at different times of day. For example, the thermostat could be set for 58° from 11 p.m. until 7 a.m. and then for 70° during the daytime.

A dirty heat-exchange filter reduces the efficiency of the heating system. A missing filter is a sure sign of careless maintenance.

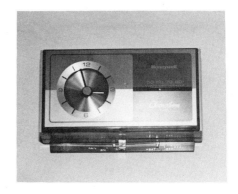

Figure 71

Check that the thermostat on-off switch works properly.

Electric Heating Systems

All electric heating systems rely on resistance heating: Coils are heated by electricity that is passed through a high-resistance wire, just like a toaster. An electrical system may take any of the forms mentioned under gas heating (forced air, wall or baseboard, or boiler) and may include heating panels that are installed above or incorporated in a sheetrock or plaster ceiling.

Electric heating is more economical to install than gas heating, since an electric system does not require a flue, gas piping, or combustion air piping. But electric heating is more expensive to operate, using vast quantities of electricity.

An electric heater should have its own fuse or circuit breaker, and the thermostat should have an automatic shut-off in case of overheating.

Solid-Fuel Heaters

Solid-fuel heaters include fireplaces, free-standing fireplace stoves (Franklin stoves), and gravity-type central units. (For advice on inspecting fireplaces and stoves, see "Fireplaces" in Chapter 2.) Houses whose primary heating system is of the solid-fuel type usually have a gas, electric, or solar back-up system.

Exhaust Systems

Exhaust fans and vents are usually to be found in bathrooms that have no windows and over kitchen ranges. They may also be used to prevent moisture buildup in attics and in bathrooms that do have windows.

The typical exhaust consists of a small electric motor-

Figure 72

Check exhaust fan for cleanliness of motor and filter. Listen for irregular motor noise that may signal a problem.

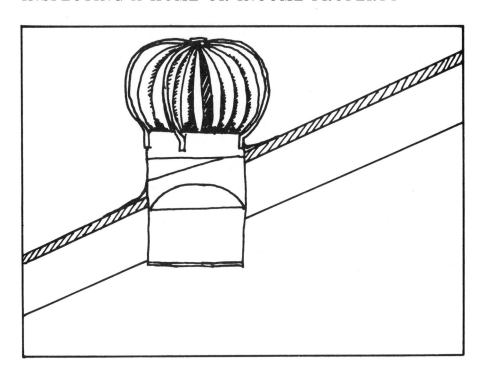

Figure 73

Attic ventilation. Proper sealant around the perimeter prevents water leakage.

driven fan and a duct that runs out through the roof or sidewall of the house (Figs. 72, 73, and 74). Island-type kitchen ranges rely on ducts that run under the floor or through the concrete slab to the outside. The newer hooded ranges are not ducted—filters in the hood trap the grease and filter the air before recirculating it back into the kitchen.

Exhaust ducts should be provided with back-draft dampers, metal or plastic flaps that reduce heat loss by closing the duct opening when the fan is off.

Evaporative Coolers

Evaporative coolers, colloquially known as "swamp coolers," are roof-mounted units used in regions of the country that have high temperatures and low relative humidity. An evaporative cooler lowers the temperature of air drawn into the house by pulling the air through water-saturated filters.

The cooler's water supply comes from the house system. The level of water in the cooler's pan or tank is controlled by a float valve, similar to that used in a toilet tank. A small pump forces the water into a perforated pipe that runs around the top of the cooler unit, and gravity then forces the water through the coarse filters and back to the supply pan. All evaporative coolers have fans and some have ducting.

While inspecting an evaporative cooler, be on the lookout for dirty filters, rusting and leaking of the pan, and discoloration of building finishes under the unit. The float

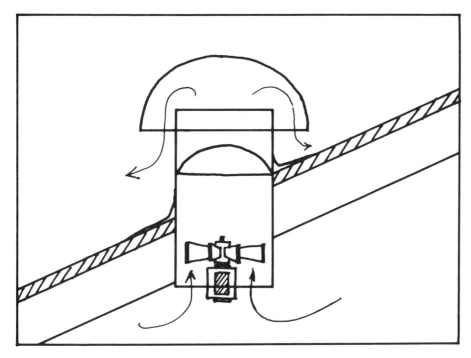

Figure 74

Attic exhaust fan. Arrows show air flow when a thermostatically controlled switch activates the fan.

valve should properly shut off the water supply when the pan or tank is filled to the correct level.

Energy Efficiency

There are three principal considerations in evaluating a house's energy efficiency: insulation, infiltration, and appliances. Insulation is discussed in Chapter 2; so here we will focus on infiltration and appliances.

Infiltration is the general term that covers all intentional and unintentional openings in the house through which heat escapes in winter and cool interior air escapes in summer. Infiltration is often the chief culprit in sky-high gas and electricity bills but almost always can be corrected in a manner that is cost-efficient. To detect sources of infiltration:

- Look for cracks or openings around tops, bottoms, and sides of window and door frames; around doors and grilles between heated living spaces and unheated spaces (garage, basement); and at wall plugs and switches.

- Make sure that the fireplace flue has a working damper and that free-standing fireplaces have tightly fitting glass or metal doors.

- Check to see that hoods and exhaust fans have back-flow dampers, and make sure that ducts from these appliances are caulked or sealed wherever they penetrate the building.

Some newer houses are truly "tight"—plastic film under the interior finish and rubber gaskets around light switches and outlets seal off the interior. Kitchen and bathroom ventilation is critical in these houses, and dehumidifiers may be needed as well, in order to prevent the buildup of moisture and stale air.

A second contributor to high energy bills are thermostats set at high levels. Lowering the thermostat on the central heating and the water heater can substantially reduce energy bills.

Also contributing to energy inefficiency are poorly adjusted, improperly installed, or antique appliances. All appliances should be tested during your inspection, of course, but your energy-efficiency evaluation will focus on:

- Heating system. Contact the local gas and electric company for an inspection of the heating system and information about energy-saving measures. Ask the inspector to help you adjust the dampers on the air ducts and registers; be sure the thermostat is functioning properly.

- Water heater. If the water heater is located in an unheated area, a water heater blanket can decrease stand-by heat loss. The blanket should not cover the air intake or the controls at the bottom of the heater. Also insulate the hot water pipes in the underfloor and attic area and the 5 feet of cold water input pipe closest to the water heater. Have the local gas company check the burner efficiency.

Energy-efficient appliances and devices include:
- intermittent-ignition gas ranges
- electric ignition furnaces
- time-controlled thermostats
- low-flow shower heads
- fluorescent lighting
- solar water heaters
- movable, insulated window coverings
- attic cooling and ventilating fans

Use this page for your own notes and questions.

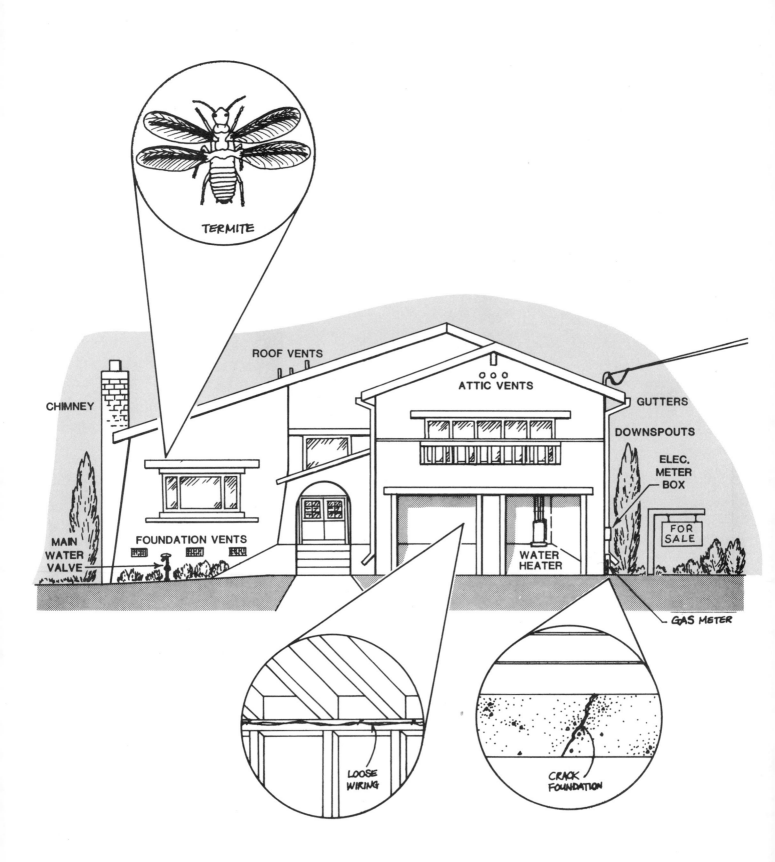

TERMITE

ROOF VENTS

ATTIC VENTS

CHIMNEY

GUTTERS

DOWNSPOUTS

ELEC.
METER
BOX

FOUNDATION VENTS

FOR
SALE

MAIN
WATER
VALVE

WATER
HEATER

GAS METER

LOOSE
WIRING

CRACK
FOUNDATION

6

Apartment House Inspection Procedures

The inspection of income property requires a broad knowledge of ordinances and standards that relate to health, safety, and maintenance. In most jurisdictions annual apartment inspections are conducted by the building, public works, or health departments. Landlords are assessed an annual fee for this service. In addition, local fire departments conduct periodic fire-safety inspections of multifamily dwellings.

The guidelines presented in this chapter are designed to help you spot existing or potential problems. All such problems should be referred to a properly trained professional. Of course, the procedures mentioned in earlier chapters are also appropriate for the inspection of apartment houses. Many of those points are treated only summarily here.

A thorough inspection of an apartment house should include:

Roof

Public hallways

Individual units

Basement and garage

Grounds

Swimming pool area

Recreation areas

Shop maintenance room

Storage compartments

Sprinkler system

Figure 75

Check ridge at top of wood shake roof for evenness.

Roof

First, know the type of roof you are inspecting. Is it a tar-and-gravel roof, composition shingle, shake, tile, or wood shingle? (For details on various roofing materials, see Chapter 2.) During your inspection, try to avoid walking on the roof.

With a ladder braced against the eaves, look at the entire roof. Check a tar-and-gravel roof for missing gravel, air bubbles on the tar paper, and blocked drain openings. Check the gutters for rusting, holes, and any other type of damage. Be sure that adjacent tree branches are not resting on the roof.

Always check the vents, valleys at the ridge line, and chimneys where changes in the roof line are prominent (Fig. 75). Make sure attic vents are not blocked from leaves and other forms of debris. Check the metal flashing for rusting. Check all flues for damaged or rusted vent caps.

Electric wires from the utility pole to the house should not be resting on the roof. Is the service head on the roof (conduit pipe connecting electric wiring to the house) sturdy?

Always check the eaves and fascia boards around the perimeter of the roof for dry rot or fungus accumulation.

Ask the local building department about requirements for fire-retardant roofing.

If there is a laundry drying platform or roof deck on top of the roof, wires and ropes for the clothesline and television antennas should be above the roof. This is a safety precaution to prevent firefighters from tripping over or being cut by low wires.

The floors of the drying platform or roof deck should be covered with approved fireproof material, fire-retardant roofing, or 24-gauge galvanized iron. Proper drainage is usually provided through the side walls of the deck or platform or by floor drains protected with screening or another similar device (Fig. 76). Exceptions to these guidelines are floors constructed with tight-fitting boards such as tongue-and-groove lumber of other solid surfacing.

The flue caps should be secure, and neither these caps nor the chimney should show deterioration from rust.

A stable railing around a roof vent shaft should be present to prevent people from falling down the vent shaft.

A penthouse door should be fireproofed and have a door closer that works properly and opens outwards. These precautions will prevent smoke and fire from coming back into the building.

Figure 76

Ponding on tar-and-gravel roof is due to poor drainage and pitch of roof.

Public Hallways

Hallway Lighting

Public hallways, corridors, stairs, passageways, and garages should be adequately lighted. All light fixtures should be in working order.

Are there directional Exit signs near stairways and fire escapes at the front, rear, and sides of the building?

Check with the fire department to find out the requirements for installation of a fire-alarm system. A fire-alarm system may be required if the building has three or more stories of occupancy and sixteen or more units. If the building has a fire-alarm system, find out if the system is connected to the police, fire, or other departments (Fig. 77).

Stairways

Handrails, guardrails, and steps should be stable and in good repair.

Outdoor stairway landings should be weather-protected. Indoor stairway enclosures should be closed and unobstructed. Three-story apartment houses should have stairways enclosed in one-hour fire-resistant construction with self-closing doors.

Wherever there are four or more risers, the current code states a handrail is needed. Be sure handrail brackets are sturdy.

If nonslip materials are installed on steps or in hallways, be sure they are secure and flush to steps or landings (Fig. 78). Nails popping up through steps should be removed.

As a safety precaution, to prevent children from falling through open *interior* or *exterior* stairway railings, guardrails should have intermediate rails, ornamental design, or other barriers so that a sphere of 6 inches in diameter cannot pass through (Fig. 79).

Figure 77

Fire alarm. Make sure the alarm does actually summon the fire or police department.

Figure 78

Missing (nonslip) rubber step covering represents a potentially serious safety hazard.

Figure 79

Top stairway balcony landing has openings in excess of 6 inches, a serious safety hazard. The openings in the bottom balcony landing are closed off with plywood.

Elevator

A public elevator should have a warning sign that advises tenants and visitors not to use the elevator in case of fire (Fig. 80). An inspection certificate should be present inside the elevator car. Inspection is annual.

Check landings on each floor to make sure that when the elevator opens its floor is level with the landing.

Fire Extinguishers

Approved fire extinguishers must be provided by the owners of the building. Fire extinguishers are inspected annually by the fire department. Recharge tags must be current (Fig. 81).

Figure 80

Safety signs should be posted near the elevator button.

Figure 81

Fire hoses should be examined for damage or missing nozzles. Check the tag on a fire extinguisher for its recharge date. Extinguishers must be recharged annually.

If in doubt, ask the local fire department about minimum size and type of fire extinguishers required for the building in question.

It's also wise to check the fire hoses located in the fire extinguisher cages along public hallways and in garage/carport areas to see if nozzles are missing or if hoses have been damaged or left wet.

Corridors (used here interchangeably with "Hallways")

Whenever more than ten residents occupy any floor above the first story, the building needs to have two exits arranged so that it is possible to reach an exit in either direction from any point in a corridor except for dead-end corridors less than 20 feet in length. Check with the building department if this appears to be a problem.

Interior Public Hallways

The walls and ceilings along the hallways should not be damp, water stained or have holes or cracks. Are the walls and ceilings in need of painting? Is there loose or missing plaster on the walls and ceilings? Do you notice any wear and tear along the public hallway carpeting, flooring, etc.? Check the flooring or carpeting for holes, cracks, or buckling.

Some jurisdictions require sprinkler systems in public hallways.

Smoke Detectors

Are there smoke detectors or smoke alarm systems along the public hallways and heat sensors in the inner courts (Fig. 82)?

Figure 82

Left: *An electrical permit is required for electrically wired smoke detector. Contact the local building department for a permit.*

Below: *Battery-operated smoke detector should be checked to be sure battery is no more than one year old.*

Window Grilles and Door Grilles

Each bedroom below the fourth story must have at least one exterior door or window that can be used for emergency exiting. Exit windows must open at least 20 inches wide by 24 inches with a minimum area of 5.7 square feet. The window sill for this exit window must be no more than 44 inches above the floor. Any bars or protective screens on these windows must be operable from the inside without need for a key or tool.

Rodents and Vermin Infestation

Look for evidence of pest infestations (see Chapter 7). Ask the present owner for records of inspections or treatments by pest control contractors. Is there a regular program of spraying and maintenance, or does the owner order pest control work only when tenants complain?

Individual Units

Are the heating facilities in good condition? Do they work properly? Are all the gas appliances (gas stoves, heater, water heaters) provided with flues and connectors? Is the main shut-off valve for each gas appliance accessible and in good working condition?

Are the floors in the kitchen and bathroom waterproofed? Bare floor boards are not accepted as waterproofed.

Does the flooring or carpeting show evidence of holes, cracks, or missing sections?

Deadbolt Locks

Each unit should have a deadbolt lock on all exit doors. These must open from the inside without the need of a key or buzzer.

Sliding Glass Doors

Doors should open and close easily. Locking devices should be in good working condition. Make sure the door is running on its proper track. Glass should be properly insulated around the door and secure in its aluminum frame. Safety tempered glass is required—look for the insignia at the bottom corner of the door (Fig. 83).

Figure 83

Sliding glass doors should be made of safety tempered glass. Check for insignia at base of door.

Appliances

It is recommended there be at least two wall plug receptacles in the kitchen and one wall plug and light fixture in each other room.

Are the light switches and light fixtures in good working condition? Plug an appliance or lamp or circuit tester into each wall receptacle to see if the receptacle works.

Check all burners of an electric stove by turning dials to the on position. See if all burners turn red. Turn on the oven dial and see if the oven works. Check control dials for all burners and oven. Lift up burners to see if the area underneath the burners is accessible for proper cleaning. Wall plug and outlet coverplate should not be damaged.

If a gas stove is present, make sure gas shut-off valve is easily accessible. If the gas stove requires a vent, make sure the oven exhaust duct from the appliance is vented properly.

Bathroom

The wash basin should be secured to the wall. Is the toilet tank cracked or damaged? Is the toilet secured to the floor with two bolts at bottom?

Some bathrooms require mechanical ventilation in lieu of a window to provide proper ventilation.

What is the condition of the tub shower? Are the ceramic or fiberglass walls in good condition? Do the faucets for the tub shower or wash basin leak? Is the floor waterproofed? Are there cracks or tiles missing on the flooring? How fast do the tub shower and wash basin drain?

Turn on the hot water in the wash basin and see how long it takes to get hot. Is there adequate water pressure?

Check the tub shower door, if there is one. Does the door open and shut properly? Do you see the words *tempered glass* at the corner of the shower door? If not, then the shower door is not made of tempered glass and could break during an accident.

Heating Facilities

Are heating facilities provided for each dwelling unit? Do the heating facilities have the proper gas connections and accessibility to the shut-off valve handle?

Kitchen

Check the condition of the kitchen sink drainboards. If there is a waste disposal, check to see if it works properly. Does the electrical wiring under the kitchen sink cabinet appear safe?

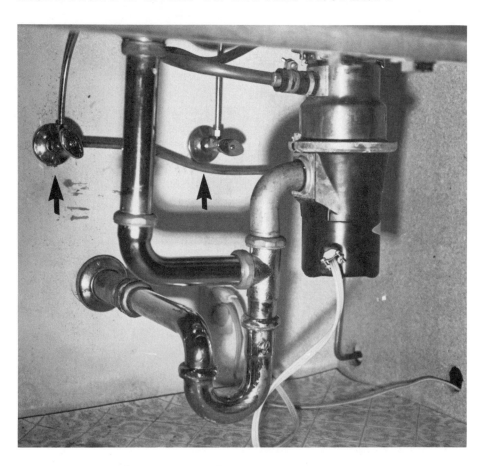

Figure 84

Water shut-off handles should open and close properly. The hole surrounding the wiring (bottom, right) is in violation of code.

Check under the kitchen sink cabinet for possible dampness on the cabinet walls and bottom (Fig. 84). Dampness could mean the P trap for waste pipe or supply lines for the hot and cold water sides is leaking. Touch the piping after you turn the water on for a minute.

Bedrooms

Are the walls and ceilings in good condition? Note any water stains or cracks. Do the closet doors open and close properly? Are the doors on track?

Check the window frames for dry rot. Are the wood sash windows easy to open and close? Are the sash cords intact? Are the windows aligned properly? If they are aluminum windows, check for proper flashing or counterflashing.

Check flooring for buckling.

A smoke detector should be located in the hallway near the bedrooms. Some areas of the country require smoke detectors in other parts of the house as well. Check with the fire department or the building department.

Utility Room

Some apartment units have a utility room where the laundry tub is located. Check the faucets and condition of the P trap for the laundry tub tray.

Basement and Garage

Garage walls (and ceilings if there's living space above) should be at least 5/8-inch sheetrock.

Check the walls and ceilings of garages, carports, and detached buildings for holes and large cracks. Determine if the holes on the walls were caused by automobile parking. Holes in the ceiling or walls could have been caused by plumbing repair work that entailed cutting a hole adjacent to the piping.

Automatic Garage Door Opener

Check evenness of the garage door when it is raised or lowered. Does remote control device for garage door work properly? Listen to door motor for scratchy or straining noises.

Check the laundry room for proper maintenance and cleanliness. Are the walls and ceilings in good condition? Check the wall receptacle plug outlet, light switch, and coverplate. If the dryer is electric, there should be a 220-volt wall receptacle plug outlet (Fig. 85).

Make sure the standpipe behind the washer and dryer is properly trapped and vented.

Whenever there are gas-fired appliances, be sure that there are some type of vent screens or openings to the exterior that supply combustion air to the appliance.

Garbage Disposal Facilities

Determine the arrangements for garbage and refuse disposal: garbage chute, garbage dumpster, or garbage cans.

If there is a garbage chute, the hoppers on each floor should be in good repair and there should not be any holes or cracks along the hoppers down to the main garbage

Figure 85

220-volt wall receptacle for electric dryer.

chute room. The garbage chute room should have an automatic fire sprinkler head and the doors to the room should be self-closing.

Garbage dumpsters should be accessible and easy to maintain. Check with the garbage company for advice.

Garbage cans and lids should be in good condition. If the garbage cans are located in a room, the door should have a self-closing device and proper ventilation.

Storage Rooms

Paint or other combustibles should not be placed in rooms with water heaters or furnaces. Storage rooms should be free of any gas-fired appliances.

Ratproofing

Does the ground of the subfloor crawl space have 2 inches of concrete poured over the soil? Some jurisdictions require such ratproofing—ask the local building department.

Underfloor Access Cover Door

The foundation access cover door should be in good condition. Open the door and check if crawl space is free of debris and rubbish.

Water Heater, Gas-Fired

A water heater located in a garage or in an enclosed closet in the garage needs adequate ventilation. Check the water heater's interior shell for damage and rust.

Figure 86

Example of a sidewalk that has been uprooted and could cause pedestrians to trip and fall. Property owners should report such dangerous conditions to the public works department.

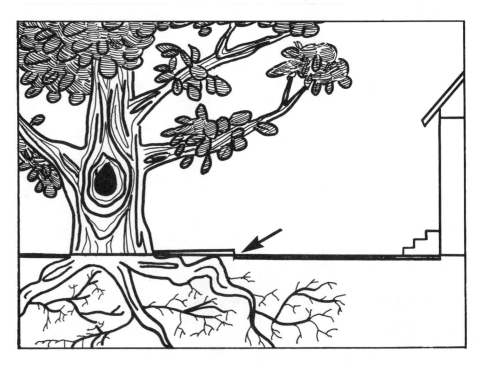

Make sure the unit has a pressure-relief valve and a drainpipe that allow water to flow out of the water heater. The venting system, vent connectors, vent diverter, and vent flues should be checked for stability.

Grounds

Sidewalks

Check the sidewalk paving at the front, rear, and sides of the building. Are there holes, cracks, or eruptions of the exterior walkways? Property owners are responsible for reporting cracks and holes to the local public works department. In the absence of such notification, property owners are liable for accidents caused by uneven or deteriorating pavement (Fig. 86).

Exterior Windows

Inspect for proper weather protection of the exterior window glass. Check double-hung windows for glazing around the window glass. Is the glazing putty brittle and falling apart? Are the wood frames in need of repair or replacement? Broken window glass should be replaced.

Stationary exterior windows should be checked for continous weather-protective sealing or glazing. If glazing appears brittle or damaged, repair may be necessary. Check interior of stationary windows under window sills to determine if wood is damp or brittle to the touch. If so, water from outside of the house may be seeping in and damaging the wood.

Exterior Paint and Weather Protection

Check exterior stucco for cracks and holes. Rub your hand over the stucco paint; if paint chalks off easily, it may not be adhering properly to the building.

Check wood buildings for loose nails on the boards and deterioration or dry rot on all wood and exterior trim.

Retaining Wall

Check all retaining walls for cracks, openings, or damages (Fig. 87). If in doubt about whether a retaining wall is in adequate condition, consult the building department.

Exterior Deck

Check the condition of the flooring. Are the floor boards in need of a new paint job? Are the floor boards loose or are nails protruding from the boards?

What type of drain is used to eliminate the water from the floor deck?

Sewer Clean-out Drain

At the perimeter of the building, locate the sewer clean-out drain. A clean-out cap should be attached to the sewer drain (Fig. 88).

Figure 87

Retaining wall at rear of building should be examined for cracks.

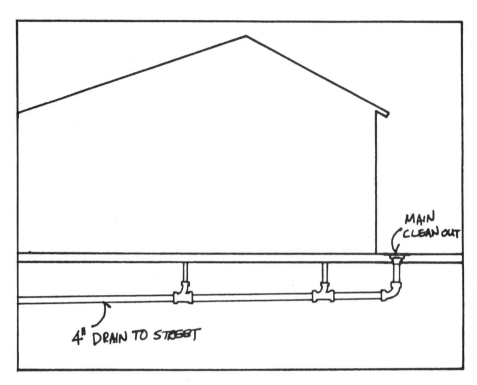

MAIN CLEAN OUT

4" DRAIN TO STREET

Figure 88

The sewer cleanout drain should be capped.

Swimming Pool Area

A swimming pool located on the grounds of an apartment building or condominium is required to meet a variety of safety regulations.

Enclosure.   The pool must be surrounded by a fence, portions of building wall, or some other strong, stable enclosure that is at least 4 feet high. Openings in the enclosure may not exceed 4 inches in diameter except for openings that are protected by doors or gates. Each door or gate must be equipped with a self-closing and self-latching device that will keep the entrance closed whenever the pool is not in use. This safety lock or latch must be at least 3-1/2 feet above the ground.

Signage.   Signs regarding policies for use of the pool, emergency first aid procedures, and emergency phone numbers must be prominently posted. Required in addition, as appropriate, are signs warning that no lifeguard is on duty, prohibiting diving in shallow pools, and cautioning children against using the pool without the supervision of an adult (Fig. 89).

Safety equipment.   Required safety equipment includes a rescue pole and a life ring. The rescue pole should be at least 12 feet long, of light and strong material, and with a blunt end or rescue hook. The life ring must be at least 17 inches in outside diameter and equipped with a 3/16-inch line long enough to span the maximum width of the pool.

Water quality.   In some jurisdictions the city or county health department conducts periodic water-quality inspections of pools. Pool operators are responsible for maintaining daily records of maintenance procedures, water-quality measures (disinfectant residue, pH), and chemical treatments administered.

Walkways.   Swimming pools should be provided with nonslip paved walkways or decking (Fig. 90). Walkways and decking should be unobstructed and should not drain into the swimming pool or overflow gutter.

Electricity and wiring.   Exterior receptacle outlets should be encased in a watertight box and properly U-grounded (Fig. 90). Bare wires are unacceptable.

Figure 89

Various safety signs must be posted in plain view in public swimming pool areas. In addition to the rules and policies that govern use of the pool, there should be:

A sign listing telephone numbers of the nearest ambulance, hospital, and fire or police rescue service.

A sign illustrating artificial respiration procedures.

At pools whose maximum depth is less than 6 feet: A sign, lettering at least 4 inches high, stating No Diving Allowed.

At pools that do not have lifeguard service: A sign, lettering at least 4 inches high, stating Warning, No Lifeguard on Duty.

At pools that allow children: A sign stating Children Should Not Use Pool Without an Adult in Attendance.

After you have inspected for compliance with these safety regulations, you should also check the following:

- Diving board should be anchored to the swimming pool.
- The pool should have at least one ladder.
- Handrails and ladder should be properly secured to the deck.
- Pool gutters should be intact and in good repair.
- Water depths should be clearly indicated (Fig. 90).
- Skimmers, chlorinators, pumps, and filters should be in good condition.
- Solar heat blanket should not have any holes and should cover the entire pool surface.

Figure 90

Above: *Check the coving around the rim of the pool. Concrete walkway should be even with coving.*

Center: *Exterior U-grounded receptacle. Cover caps have water-tight seals.*

Right: *Pool should have clearly marked pool depth indicators.*

Manufactured Homes (Mobile Homes)

Most jurisdictions allow manufactured housing (mobile homes) to be installed on compatible lots zoned for single-family housing. These factory-built homes must be installed on a permanent foundation and anchored to the ground.

The mobile home owner must obtain a building permit and pay all relevant fees and costs for sewerage, water connection, and the like. The home is subject to local property taxes based on its assessed market value.

A mobile home is subject to the same development standards as a single-family dwelling, including standards for enclosures, access, vehicle parking, and minimum area requirements. Requirements specific to mobile homes include:

- Every outside door must have steps and handrails.
- Foundation supports or piers (usually concrete building blocks) must stabilize the home so that it is level.
- The wheels must be concealed by skirting that does not impede access or ventilation.

All mobile homes built for sale in the United States after June 15, 1976, are required to meet standards established by the federal Department of Housing and Urban Development (HUD). Units built before this national standard took effect should have a HUD tag.

Ask the local building department about zoning regulations, registration, and other requirements. In California, for example, mobile homes that are to be placed on single-family lots must be at least 8 feet wide and 32 feet long, excluding hitches.

Condominiums

Prospective condominium owners should completely familiarize themselves with all their responsibilities and liabilities as owners. For example, if your unit is damaged by a leak in an upstairs neighbor's bathroom, who is responsible for the repair costs?

New owners will be required to sign the condominium's CCR (conditions, covenants, and restrictions). Read this legally binding document carefully—consult with an attorney if necessary. Don't take anything for granted and don't assume anything that is not in writing.

Inquire about whether an owners' association has been formed and try to determine whether management and the owners are cooperative. Ask about maintenance of the commons areas: grounds, elevators, pool, and recreation areas.

Your on-site inspection should include all the items mentioned earlier in book, but pay special attention to:

Walls. Check the construction of all party walls (walls that separate adjoining units). In newer condominiums party walls are usually insulated double walls. Many older condominiums, however, have single walls and noise carries between units. If there is a crawl space, check to see whether the walls extend all the way down to the ground. Such walls prevent fire from spreading from one unit to the next.

Utilities. Is each unit provided with its own water heater, heating system, and thermostat? Or are utilities centrally controlled?

Lighting. Always check for adequate lighting along the exterior areas of the building, especially in the garage or carport, the public hallways and stairways, and the laundry room.

Swimming pool. If there is a swimming pool, ask about policies pertaining to its use.

Use this page for your own notes and questions.

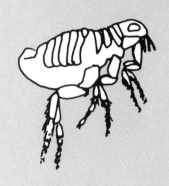

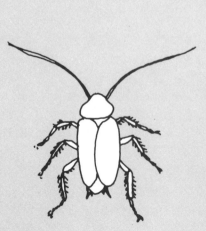

7

Structural Termite Reports & Pest Control

Whenever the sale of a residential property is in escrow, a state-licensed structural pest control inspector (commonly called a "termite inspector") must examine the property.

Before the inspection, the prospective buyer should ask the seller or tenant to make accessible for inspection all areas that are locked or blocked by storage of furniture and heavy objects.

Written inspection reports are documents of public record, and anyone can request copies of a report from the state structural pest control board. The board will also have on file recent notices of completion of pest control work.

Reading a Structural Pest Control Report

Each state has a standard report form (a California form is shown in Fig. 91). Here is a brief description of the types of problems that are noted on these reports.

Subterranean termites. Subterranean termites build nests in the soil and then burrow into wood that is in contact with the soil. Moisture (from plumbing leaks or sprinklers) and inadequate subfloor ventilation aggravate the situation. Symptoms of subterranean termite infestation include:

- cracking of foundation or slab floors under walls
- mud tubes on foundation, piers, sewer pipes
- irregular, bumpy, or discolored paint
- unsound wood under paint
- windows that do not open and close properly

To control subterranean termites, all tubes between soil and wood must be destroyed, subfloor ventilation should be improved, plumbing leaks and other sources of moisture should be repaired, and all wood should be protected from direct contact with soil. Faulty grading that allows the soil level to rise above the level of the foundation sill must also be corrected.

Drywood termites. Drywood termites can live in wood without any contact with soil. Their droppings resemble angular grains or sandlike pellets. Infested wood makes a rattling sound when shaken. You may also detect small holes in paint.

Control of drywood termites is by fumigation. In addition, improvements in ventilation in attics, garages, subflooring, and wall spaces (especially around windows) are advisable.

Dampwood termites. Dampwood termites favor moist spots near walkways, bathrooms, plumbing leaks, porches, exterior stairways, and the like. Control of dampwood termites entails breaking soil-wood contacts and eliminating sources of leaks.

Wood-destroying fungi. Wood-destroying fungi are plants that grow into wood. They need some moisture and warmth for germination. Painting and caulking the exterior of the home should supply adequate protection.

Powder post beetles. Powder post beetles invade wood derived from broadleaf plants. Improperly cured wood furniture, window trim, and picture frames are the most typical sites of infestation. Evidence of infestation includes the presence of a very fine talclike wood dust. Infested wood should be removed from the dwelling and either fumigated or disposed of.

Carpenter ants. Carpenter ants are very common in wooded rural regions. They usually do not invade sound wood, but their mining can destroy structures built of pine. Adequate control involves chemical spraying by licensed pest control workers; fumigation is not necessary.

The pest control inspector will also note instances of earth-wood contacts, shower stall leaks, cellulose debris (scraps of leftover construction wood), and faulty grading.

Common Household Pests

The three most important questions about household pests are: Why is the pest present? How can it be eliminated? What will prevent it from returning? Here are some quick answers regarding the ten most common household pests.

Fleas

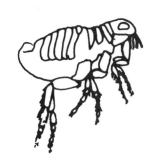

Fleas are small, usually dark-colored insects that jump rapidly away when they are discovered. Fleas are rather easy to identify: They are distinctly flat from side to side; if light-colored, they are orange or yellowed brown, but usually they are deep mahogany brown to nearly black in color.

Fleas must have a mammal host, or in rare instances a bird host, to survive. Human fleas are exceedingly rare in the United States and Western Europe. Almost all flea problems inside American homes are the result of dogs and cats. These fleas will readily bite humans but cannot reproduce on human blood.

The first point of flea control is to very carefully vacuum the corners and edges of rooms, behind and beneath furniture, and other secluded areas. Thorough vacuum cleaning eliminates flea eggs, larvae, and pupae and the larval food supply.

Control of adult fleas may require spraying chemicals on the premises. The chemicals for inside spraying are different from those used in the yard. Chemical spraying can control flea larvae for up to six months.

Cockroaches

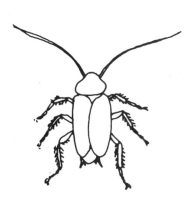

Cockroaches are also readily identifiable: They are flat from top to bottom and very wide for their height; their legs are large and spiny. Some cockroaches can fly, if temperatures and humidity are high. Cockroaches can be almost any color.

Cockroaches require high humidity and warm environments. If the house is dry and cool, cockroaches will be limited to kitchen, bathroom, and washing areas. If the house is very dark, humid and warm, cockroaches will do well throughout. Since cockroaches need food, good sanitation practices may greatly restrict them.

Temperature and moisture control are very important

in preventing cockroach infestations. No amount of pesticides will do the job in buildings where conditions are poor. However, a special new chemical, juvenile hormone promises long-term control.

Roof Rats

In recent years the roof rat has become more common in suburban neighborhoods in temperate regions. Roof rats readily enter attics, garages, wall spaces, and subfloor areas but do not usually nest in the house. To control rats one needs to find the rat's entry-exit hole and repair it during the day, while the rats are usually outdoors. If sealed in by the repair work, rats are vulnerable to trapping with a spring snap-trap. Place the baited trap where the rats are active, but do not set the trap's trigger until the bait has been taken at least once. Moistened oat flakes make good bait. Poisons should not be used inside a home until traps have been tried, because the rats may die from the poisons in places where they cannot be removed, which will cause very bad odors and possibly problems with mites.

House Mice

House mice look like small rats, but mice spend virtually all their time in the kitchen or other areas where food is available. Their entry holes are usually within a few inches of the ground outside the building.

Control of mice begins with sanitation—all food materials must be protected. Once their food supply is curtailed, mice can be readily trapped or caught on glueboards. Poisoned bait can be used more freely for mice, because odors are not as large a problem.

Carpet Beetles

Most carpet beetles are small, round to oblong, with whitish undersides. The larvae of the beetle are very hairy, resembling small clumps of fur.

Good sanitation, especially vacuum cleaning, will keep carpet beetles in check. However, they will sometimes infest high-protein foods that have been stored for long periods of time. Foods that are rarely used should be carefully stored under dry conditions. Once a package is open, dry foods absorb moisture from the air and become vulnerable if they are stored in warm moist areas such as upper cupboards. Carpet beetles may also infest woolen or leather goods, especially if they are damp. Wool clothing should be thoroughly dry before being put into storage for the summer.

Chemicals, if properly used, can be of much greater help in controlling carpet beetles than in controlling most other insect problems in the house.

Ants

Very few species of ants nest indoors. They always travel in large numbers and usually trail each other.

Ants can be only marginally inhibited by sanitation, and chemical control is almost always necessary. Fortunately, control of ants can usually be done in the yard. However, if the ants are minute and yellowish to reddish in color, control in the house will be necessary and should be left to professionals.

Meal Moths

If you see small moths flying in the kitchen area or other areas where food materials are kept, catch one. If the outer half of the front wing is much darker than the rest of the moth, it is an Indian meal moth.

Moth larvae produce a great deal of webbing and heavy infestations will cause food to clump in one mass or hang in stringy masses. All grain and grain-derived foods, nuts, seeds, dried fruits, pasta, chocolate, dry pet foods, bird seeds, and grass seeds can become infested.

The Indian meal moth cannot be controlled by chemicals; its larvae infest areas that can be reached only by extensive fumigation.

Infested materials should be disposed of or cleared of moth eggs and larvae by freezing or heating above 140° F. Good sanitation and proper storage of foods will prevent infestation.

Grain Beetles

The most common food pest is a small long, red-brown beetle called the saw-toothed grain beetle. This beetle infests grain and grain products (flour, meal) that are improperly stored. The saw-toothed grain beetle requires moisture. Some of the larger beetle pests can live only in food already infested with mildew-type fungi.

The only control for grain beetles is good sanitation and proper food storage. Areas where baking is done should be thoroughly vacuumed to prevent infestation. Very serious infestations of food-storage areas may require fumigation by licensed professionals. Unless good sanitation is continuous, reinfestation will occur.

House Dust Mites

The material referred to as house dust is a complex of mostly organic materials: pollen, fungus spores, and human skin and hair. This material is a rich food substrate for mites. The type of mites present depends to a large extent on the constituents of the dust and the humidity.

House dust mites may cause serious problems for some people—many "dust allergies" are actually allergies to house dust mites. Typical allergic reactions include respiratory problems and skin rashes.

Chemical application by professional pest control workers may give temporary relief. But the mites will come back if sanitation lapses. In extreme cases, items of heavily soiled furniture may have to be discarded.

Honey Bees

When honey bees nest in close proximity to people they can be dangerous, and bee stings can sometimes be fatal. Bee nests inside of structures can also cause considerable structural damage.

Some beekeepers will remove bees from a house. If you cannot locate a beekeeper, a professional pest control company may be required. Approach a bee nest with great caution. Once the bees are gone the holes giving access to the structure must be sealed. It may be necessary to clean out the hive material (wax, honey, dead bees, pollen, larvae) before sealing up the holes.

One must always be aware that the presence of any pest inside a house indicates that something is amiss. Small flying insects may mean that sanitation is at fault or that the house is not tight. Pests such as mice, rats, birds, or other larger animals indicate that the external pest proofing is not intact. Structural pests such as termites expose structural defects. Any unusual odor in a house should be explained. Some pests such as cockroaches, rats, bats, etc. give a particular smell. Smells of mildew, mustiness, or chemicals, especially combined with new paint or carpeting odors may indicate an attempt to mask problems.

Figure 91

Pest Control Reports

STANDARD STRUCTURAL PEST CONTROL INSPECTION REPORT
(WOOD-DESTROYING PESTS OR ORGANISMS)
This is an inspection report only - not a Notice of Completion.

ADDRESS OF PROPERTY INSPECTED	BLDG. NO. 123	STREET America Avenue	CITY America CO. CODE	DATE OF INSPECTION June 26, 1989

Affix stamp here on Board copy only

↓ **A LICENSED PEST CONTROL** ↓
OPERATOR IS AN EXPERT IN
HIS FIELD. ANY QUESTIONS
RELATIVE TO THIS REPORT
SHOULD BE REFERRED TO HIM.

FIRM LICENSE NO.	CO. REPORT NO. (if any)	STAMP NO.

Inspection Ordered by (Name and Address) _Ace High Realty, 220 Main Street, Los Altos, CA 94022_
Report Sent to (Name and Address) _Ace High Realty, 220 Main Street, Los Altos, CA 94022_
Owner's Name and Address _R. G. Blair, 123 America Avenue, America, CA 99922_
Name and Address of a Party in Interest _None_
INSPECTED BY: _Termite Routers_   LICENSE NO. _6827_   Original Report ☒   Supplemental Report ☐   Number of Pages 2

YES	CODE	SEE DIAGRAM BELOW	YES	CODE	SEE DIAGRAM BELOW	YES	CODE	SEE DIAGRAM BELOW	YES	CODE	SEE DIAGRAM BELOW
X	S-Subterranean Termites			B-Beetles-Other Wood Pests			Z-Dampwood Termites		X	EM-Excessive Moisture Condition	
X	K-Dry-Wood Termites		X	FG-Faulty Grade Levels		X	SL-Shower Leaks		X	IA-Inaccessible Areas	
X	F-Fungus or Dry Rot			EC-Earth-wood Contacts			CD-Cellulose Debris			FI-Further Inspection Recom.	

1. SUBSTRUCTURE AREA (soil conditions, accessibility, etc.) Family room area inaccessible
2. Was Stall Shower water tested? Yes   Did floor coverings indicate leaks? Yes
3. FOUNDATIONS (Type, Relation to Grade, etc.) Satisfactory
4. PORCHES . . . STEPS . . . PATIOS   Front and patio porches require treatment
5. VENTILATION (Amount, Relation to Grade, etc.) Satisfactory. Entry door missing.
6. ABUTMENTS . . . Stucco walls, columns, arches, etc. Wooden fence attached to house
7. ATTIC SPACES (accessibility, insulation, etc.) Extensive drywood termite infestation
8. GARAGES (Type, accessibility, etc.) Floor of concrete slab is cracked
9. OTHER   Subterranean termites common in old tree stumps in rear yard

DIAGRAM AND EXPLANATION OF FINDINGS (This report is limited to structure or structures shown on diagram.)

General Description _Single story, wood frame, stucco covered California "ranch style" house._

Certain areas are recognized by the industry as inaccessible and/or for other reasons not inspected. These include but are not limited to: inaccessible and/or, insulated attics or portions thereof, attics with less than 18" clear crawl space, the interior of hollow walls; spaces between a floor or porch deck and the ceiling below; areas where there is no access without defacing or tearing out lumber, masonry or finished work; areas behind stoves, refrigerators or beneath floor coverings, furnishings; areas where encumbrances and storage, conditions or locks make inspection impractical; and areas or timbers around eaves that would require use of an extension ladder.
Slab floor construction has become more prevalent in recent years. Floor coverings may conceal cracks in the slab that will allow infestations to enter. Infestations in the walls may be concealed by plaster so that a diligent inspection may not uncover the true condition. These areas are not practicable to inspect because of health hazzards, damage to the structure; or inconvenience. They were not inspected unless described in this report. We recommend further inspection if there is any question about the above noted areas. Re: Structural Pest Control Act, Article6, Section 8516 (b), paragraph 1990 (j). Amended, effective March 1, 1974.

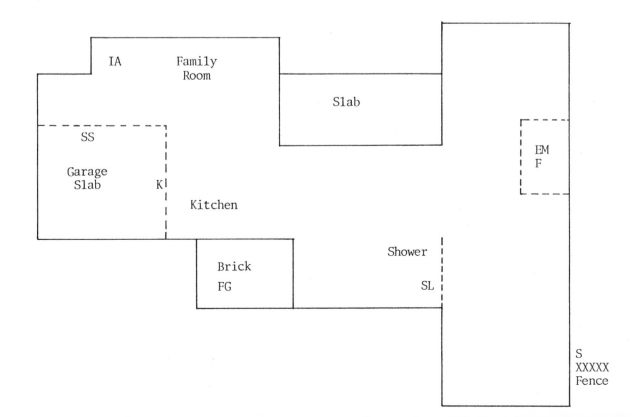

FIELD WORK SHEET —

Date of Request ___June 25, 1989___
Date of Inspection ___June 26, 1989___

BLDG. NO.	STREET	CITY	CODE NUMBER
123	America Avenue	America	

Inspection Ordered by (Name and Address) ... Ace High Realty, 220 Main, Los Altos, CA 94022
Report Sent to (Name and Address) .... Ace High Realty, 220 Main, Los Altos, CA 94022
Owner's Name and Address ... ... R. G. Blair, 123 America Avenue, America, CA 99922
Name and Address of a Party in Interest .... None

INSPECTED BY: Termite Routers

LICENSE NO.	This is an	This is a	Number of Pages
6827	Original Report ☒	Supplemental Report ☐	of this Report ___2___

YES	CODE	SEE DIAGRAM BELOW	YES	CODE	SEE DIAGRAM BELOW	YES	CODE	SEE DIAGRAM BELOW	YES	CODE	SEE DIAGRAM BELOW
X	S—Subterranean Termites			B—Beetles—Other Wood Pests			Z—Dampwood Termites		X	EM—Excessive Moisture Condition
X	K—Dry-Wood Termites		X	FG—Faulty Grade Levels		X	SL—Shower Leaks		X	IA—Inaccessible Areas
X	F—Fungus or Dry Rot			EC—Earth-wood Contacts			CD—Cellulose Debris			FI—Further Inspection Recom.

1. SUBSTRUCTURE AREA (soil conditions, accessibility, etc.)
Family room addition built over former garage and patio too narrow to crawl.

2. Was Stall Shower water tested?   Did floor coverings indicate leaks?
Yes. Discolored, buckled linoleum in MB bath and hall bath.

3. FOUNDATIONS (Type, Relation to Grade, etc.)
Satisfactory

4. PORCHES . . . STEPS . . . PATIOS
Front brick porch and back patio porch must be drilled and treated.

5. VENTILATION (Amount, Relation to Grade, etc.)
Satisfactory, however, crawl space entry cover is missing.

6. ABUTMENTS . . . Stucco walls, columns, arches, etc.
Wooden fence attached to SW corner has subterranean termites.

7. ATTIC SPACES (accessibility, insulation, etc.)
Rafters, joists, bracing, roof sheeting in garage has drywood termite infestation.

8. GARAGES (Type, accessibility, etc.)
Garage slab cracked allowing subterranean termites access to framing.

9. OTHER
Extensive subterranean termite activity in old stumps in back yard.

DIAGRAM AND EXPLANATION OF FINDINGS AND METHODS OF RECOMMENDED CORRECTIONS

General Description_____

2nd floor
shower _____

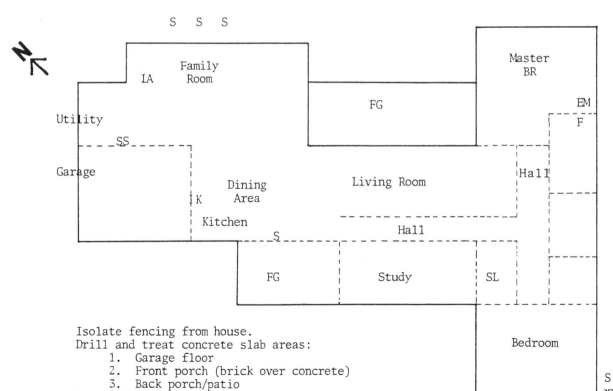

Isolate fencing from house.
Drill and treat concrete slab areas:
    1. Garage floor
    2. Front porch (brick over concrete)
    3. Back porch/patio
Tent and fumigate for roof structure drywood problem

Appendix A

Resources: Agencies & Professionals to Contact

A variety of municipal, county, and state offices provide information about building codes and housing laws and also investigate complaints made by home buyers.

Department of Real Estate (state)

- Provides information about the duties of real estate brokers and salespersons.
- Investigates consumer complaints concerning misrepresentation of material facts by real estate brokers and salespersons.

Contractor's Licensing Board (state)

- Investigates complaints about work performed by licensed contractors.
- Investigates complaints about construction performed without the required building permits.

Structural Pest Control Board (state)

- Provides copies of termite reports.
- Investigates complaints about termite inspectors and falsified inspection reports.

Division of Industrial Safety (state)

- Responsible for inspecting elevators in multifamily housing.

Department of Health (state and local)

- Provides information about maintenance, sanitation, ventilation, and occupancy of apartment houses, lodging houses, and dwellings.
- Enforces rules and regulations regarding swimming pools.

Building Department (local)

- Provides information about the erection, construction, movement, conversion, and alteration of apartment houses, lodging houses, and dwellings.
- Authorizes building permits.
- Provides files on certificates of completion for construction work performed under a building permit.

Planning and Zoning Department (local)

- Provides information about types of buildings and uses allowed in specific zoning areas.
- Reviews height limits and setbacks before building additions to existing property are approved.
- Reviews existing use of property; legal but nonconforming uses may be conceded to the current owner only.

Public Works Department (local)

- Determines whether property is encroaching on public right-of-way, private property, etc.
- Responsible for maintenance of public property.

Fire Marshal (local)

- Inspects properties for fire hazards, faulty weed abatement, and similar conditions that may endanger the health and safety of neighboring properties.
- Provides information ab193out requirements for smoke detectors, general safety, and evacuation plans.
- On request, will inspect roofing jobs.

Water Department (local)

- Provides information about water pressure, water hardness.

Assessor's Office (local)

- Maintains local map book, sale information, comparison appraisals, names and addresses of current property owners.
- Appraises properties for valuation for tax purposes.
- Maintains records of physical descriptions of land parcels and improvements (topography, square footage, room count, interior finish).

- Provides copies of original permits for buildings.
- Maintains records indicating whether work and additions performed on buildings were done under permit.

Tax Collector's Office (local)

- Maintains records of current property owners' names, mailing addresses, and date of last payment of local property taxes.

Gas and Electric Company (local)

- On request, will inspect any gas-fired appliance.
- Provides information about energy conservation measures.

Among the professionals whose assistance may be useful in evaluating a residential or income property are:

civil or structural engineer
soils and foundation engineer
general building contractor
electrical contractor
plumbing contractor
mechanical contractor
roofing contractor
swimming pool contractor
garage door company

Inspection Checklist for Residential Property

This checklist is intended only as a guideline; it should not be construed or used as an actual inspection report. Conditions that may need correcting, repairs, or replacement should be left to the discretion and judgment of the appropriate agency or professional.

EXTERIOR

	S	U	NA	Comments
Structural/Foundation				
Raised/slab—cracked, missing/damaged/continuous				
Underfloor crawl space				
Opening—obstructed/OK				
Access door				
Foundation vent screens				
Minimum 18″ clearance				
Ground/cement/dirt				
Ratproofing (soil is covered with concrete)				
Ground/cement/dirt/partial				
Bolting (mudsill to foundation)				
Earthquake bracing				
Roof				
Type:				
Condition				

S: *Satisfactory*   U: *Unsatisfactory*   NA: *Not applicable*

	S	U	NA	Comments
Gutters & downspouts				
None				
Location				
Type:				
Brackets				
Condition				
Drainage				
Exterior walls				
Stucco/wood/aluminum/bricks				
Hairline cracks				
Large cracks (1/8″ or wider)				
Brickwork—broken/loose/missing				
Paint—good/peeling/poor				
Exterior siding and wood trim				
Earth piled against siding/trim				
6″ separation of earth from wood				
Exterior windows				
Condition				
Aluminum/double hung/casement/other				
Wood sash				
Caulking				
Chimney				
Spark arrester				
Secured to wall				
Firebricks				
Mortar				
Cracks				
Metal coverplate				
Exterior stairways				
Front/rear/side				
Handrails				
Rear porch/deck				
Railing/stairway steps				
Rise 8″/Run 9″				
Handrails				

S: *Satisfactory*   U: *Unsatisfactory*   NA: *Not applicable*

	S	U	NA	Comments
Rear exterior patio overhang				
Garage				
Door—sectional/one piece/ wood/aluminum/other				
Vent screen				
Roof				
Accessory building				
Storage shed—wood/metal/other				
Location—less than 3′ from property line				
Power pole				
Fences				
Side/rear/front				
Wood/brick/other				
Retaining walls				
Cement/wood/brick				
Condition				
Guard rails				
Grading				
Ground slopes away from building/ pitched toward building/level				
Landscaping				
Lawn—front/rear				
Sprinkler system				
Shrubbery				
Electrical				
Main service panel				
Wiring in detached garage/carport				
Ampere service 30/60/100+				
Electrical weatherhead—condition				
Exterior light fixtures				
Ground/wall/ceiling				
Loose/missing/damaged				
Wall receptacle outlet				
U-grounded				
Exterior use/interior use				
GFI				

S: *Satisfactory*   U: *Unsatisfactory*   NA: *Not applicable*

	S	U	NA	Comments
Plumbing				
Main shut-off valve				
Lawn sprinkler system				
Anti-siphon device				
Vent pipes/extends 6″ above roof				
Sewer clean-outs				
Location				
Main				
Kitchen				
Cap cover				
Water heater				
Gas-fired/electric				
Location				
Capacity/gals.				
Corrosion on fittings/ flue/pressure-relief valve/drainpipe				
Draft diverter				
Water pressure				
Laundry tub or clothes washer standpipe				
Clearance to combustibles				
Adequate combustion air				
Vent rises 1/4″ per foot				
Swimming pool				
Condition				
Fencing				
Gate				
Signs posted				
Safety measures & devices				
Nonslip paved walk/deck				
Electrical wiring/receptacle plug outlets				
Lights & appliances grounded (GFI)				
Pool maintenance equipment				
Solar blanket				
Ladder & handrail				
Diving board				

S: *Satisfactory*   U: *Unsatisfactory*   NA: *Not applicable*

INTERIOR

	S	U	NA	Comments
Living room				
Condition				
Walls—panel board/wallpaper				
Ceiling—acoustical/plaster sheetrock/other				
Floor—carpeted/hardwood/asphalt/ vinyl/composition/linoleum/other				
Wall receptacle plug				
Outlets/light switches				
Light fixtures				
Windows—aluminum/double hung/ casement/iron bar grille/other				
Fireplace				
Damper/firescreen/ firebricks/mortar & grout				
Free-standing fireplace				
Heating appliance/duct/ registers/thermostat				
Dining room				
Condition				
Walls/ceiling				
Floor—carpeted/hardwood/other				
Wall receptacle plug				
Outlets/light switches				
Light fixtures				
Windows—aluminum/double hung/ casement/other				
Fireplace				
Heating appliance/duct/thermostat				
Sliding glass door				
Safety tempered glass				
Operable				
Lock present				
Insulated				
Kitchen				
Condition				

S: *Satisfactory*   U: *Unsatisfactory*   NA: *Not applicable*

	S	U	NA	Comments
Kitchen, cont'd.				
Sink drainboard/backsplash				
Sink mortar/ceramic tiles				
Faucets				
Water pressure				
Pipes bang				
P trap				
Garbage disposal				
Stove—gas/electric				
Vent				
Connection				
Shut-off valve for gas stove				
Exhaust fan & hood				
Light fixtures				
Dishwasher				
Windows—aluminum/double hung/casement/other				
Walls—condition				
Ceiling—condition				
U-ground				
Wall receptacle plug				
Outlets/switches				
Heater duct				
Infestations—rodent/roach/other				
Family room				
Condition				
Walls/ceiling				
Floor—carpet/hardwood/other				
Wall receptacle plug				
Outlets/switches				
Light fixtures				
Windows—aluminum/double hung/casement/other				
Fireplace				
Damper/bricks/mortar				
Heating appliance/duct				

S: *Satisfactory*   U: *Unsatisfactory*   NA: *Not applicable*

	S	U	NA	Comments
Family room, cont'd.				
Sliding glass door				
Safety tempered glass				
Operable				
Lock present				
Insulated				
Master bedroom				
Condition				
Walls/ceiling				
Floor—carpet/hardwood/other				
Wall receptacle plug				
Outlets/switches				
Light fixtures				
Windows—aluminum/double hung/ casement/other				
Heating appliance/duct				
Closets				
Ceiling				
Attic access cover				
Insulation				
Bedroom #2				
Condition				
Walls/ceiling				
Floor—carpet/hardwood/other				
Wall receptacle plug				
Outlets/switches				
Light fixtures				
Windows—aluminum/double hung/ casement/other				
Heating appliance/duct				
Closets				
Hall				
Smoke detector				
Walls/ceiling				
Floor—carpet/hardwood/other				
Wall receptacle plug				

S: *Satisfactory*   U: *Unsatisfactory*   NA: *Not applicable*

	S	U	NA	Comments
Hall, cont'd.				
Outlets/switches				
Light fixtures				
Skylight				
Heating appliance/duct				
Closets				
Bathroom				
Walls/ceiling				
Floor—tile/linoleum/other				
Windows—aluminum/double hung/other				
U-ground				
GFI				
Wall receptacle plug				
Outlets/switches				
Light fixtures				
Heater duct				
Toilet				
Wash basin				
Faucets/P trap				
Secured to wall				
Shut-off handles				
Tub shower				
Curtain rod/shower/enclosure/other				
Tile/other				
Condition				
Faucet				
Mechanical fan				
Insulation				
Roof: inches of insulation				
Walls: inches of insulation				
Raised floor: inches of insulation				
Garage				
Attached/detached				
One-hour fire resistant wall next to living area				

S: *Satisfactory*　　　　　U: *Unsatisfactory*　　　　　NA: *Not applicable*

	S	U	NA	Comments
Garage, cont'd.				
Hollow-core door				
Solid-core door				
Stairway railing				
Laundry tub—plastic/cement/other				
U-ground outlets/switches				
Heating system				
Wall furnace/floor furnace/forced air				
Air grilles clean				
Vent rises 1/4″ per foot				
Adequate combustion air				
Gas dryer				
Exhaust to exterior				
Cooling systems				
Clean				
Recently serviced				
Noisy/quiet				
Filters				
Connectors and accessibility				
Meets minimum heat requirements				
Utility room				
Condition				
Laundry tub—cement/plastic				
Tub stabilized/secured/ properly braced				
Separate 20-amp circuits for clothes washer				

S: *Satisfactory*   U: *Unsatisfactory*   NA: *Not applicable*

Inspection Checklist for Income Property

This checklist is intended only as a guideline; it should not be construed or used as an actual inspection report. Conditions that may need correcting, repairs, or replacement should be left to the discretion and judgment of the appropriate agency or professional.

EXTERIOR

	S	U	NA	Comments
Roof				
Type:				
Condition				
Gutters & downspouts				
None				
Location				
Type:				
Brackets				
Condition				
Drainage				
Flue caps/vents—12″ above roof top				
Skylight/attic vents/solar panels				
Electrical weatherhead—wiring				
Chimney				
Spark arrester				
Secured to wall				
Firebricks				
Mortar				
Cracks				
Metal coverplate				

S: *Satisfactory*   U: *Unsatisfactory*   NA: *Not applicable*

	S	U	NA	Comments
Vent shaft—opening protected/railing				
Penthouse door fireproofed				
Working door closer				
Attic ventilation				
Louvered				
Wire mesh				
Other				
Roof deck				
Wires on drying platform				
8′ above roof				
Stair penthouse door/closer				
Metal clad on exterior side of door				
Wooden platform/railing				
Wooden boards				
Grounds				
Foundation—cracked/missing/damaged/continuous				
Underfloor crawl space				
Opening—obstructed/OK				
Access door				
Foundation vent screens				
Minimum 18″ clearance				
Ratproofing (soil covered with concrete)				
Grading—ground slopes away from building/pitched toward building/level				
Sidewalks—front/rear/side				
Paving—front/rear/side				
Exterior light fixtures				
Ground/wall/ceiling				
Loose/missing/damaged				
Wall receptacle outlets				
U-ground				
Exterior use/interior use				
GFI				
Exterior windows				
Condition				

S: *Satisfactory*   U: *Unsatisfactory*   NA: *Not applicable*

	S	U	NA	Comments
Exterior windows, cont'd.				
Weather protection				
Framing				
Aluminum/double hung/casement/other				
Caulking				
Exterior walls				
Stucco/wood/aluminum/other				
Bricks				
Hairline cracks				
Large cracks (1/8″ or wider)				
Brickwork—broken/loose/missing				
Paint—good/peeling/poor				
Weather protection				
Siding & wood trim				
6″ separation of earth from wood				
Fences & retaining walls				
Side/rear/front				
Wood/brick/other				
Condition				
Exterior deck				
Condition				
Floor				
Drainage of water				
Sewer clean-outs				
Main				
Kitchen				
Location				
Cap				
Weather protected				
Driveway & walkway				
Drainage				
Uneven/level/damaged				
Metal coverplate for drain				
Landscaping				
Lawn—front/rear				
Sprinkler system				

S: *Satisfactory*   U: *Unsatisfactory*   NA: *Not applicable*

	S	U	NA	Comments
Landscaping, cont'd.				
Anti-siphon device				
Shrubbery				
Fence/gates—front/rear				
Fire prevention devices				
Fire sprinklers				
Fire extinguisher				
Swimming pool				
Condition				
Fencing/4 feet high				
Gate/self-closing/self-latching device				
Signs posted				
Safety measures & devices				
Nonslip paved walk/deck				
Electrical wiring/receptacle plug outlets				
Lights & appliances grounded (GFI)				
Pool maintenance equipment				
Solar blanket				
Ladder & handrail				
Diving board				
Accessory building				
Storage shed—wood/metal/other				
Location—less than 3' from property line				
Power pole				
Basement and Garage				
Garage				
Door operation				
Walls/ceilings				
One-hour fire rated material				
Laundry area				
Wall receptacle plug outlets/light/switches				
U-ground receptacles				
Dryer—gas/electric				
Automatic garage door opener				

	S	U	NA	Comments
Garbage disposal facilities				
Location				
Cans—tight fitting lids				
Chute/sprinkler head, self-closing device for door				
Dumpster				
Storage rooms				
Location				
One-hour fire construction material				
5/8″ fire code sheetrock or equivalent				
Rat proofing				
Cement				
Ground area				
Basement				
Underfloor access cover door				
Water heater, gas-fired				
Condition				
Location				
Electric				
Capacity gals.				
Proper venting				
Connectors/secured				
Draft diverter				
Corrosion on fittings/flue				
Pressure relief valve/drainpipe				
Adequate combustion air				
Clearance to combustibles				
Public hallways				
Condition				
Light fixtures operable				
Stairway enclosures—smoke barriers/ sprinkler system				
Fire extinguishers/5 lbs.				
Missing				
Current recharge tag				
Wall/stair				

	S	U	NA	Comments
Public stairways & landings				
Condition				
Loose treads & risers				
Carpet/cement/other				
Nonslip material				
Guardrails/handrails				
Stabilized/loose/missing				
Wood/metal/other				
Openings less than 6″ in diameter				
Corridors				
Condition				
Carpet/wood/other				
Dead-end corridors fire protected				
Two exits available				
Exit door has Exit sign posted				
Interior public hallways				
Wall/ceiling				
Access opening on ceiling				
Floor—carpeting/wood/other				
Entrance door				
1-3/8″ solid-core/hollow				
1″ deadbolt on apartment exit door				
Viewer on door				
Screen door				
Smoke detectors/smoke alarm system/ heat sensors				
Infestation—rodents/vermin/other				

S: *Satisfactory*   U: *Unsatisfactory*   NA: *Not applicable*

INTERIOR

	S	U	NA	Comments
Living room				
Condition				
Walls—panel board/wallpaper				
Ceiling—acoustical/plaster sheetrock/other				
Floor—carpeted/hardwood/asphalt/ vinyl/composition/linoleum/other				
Wall receptacle plug				
Outlets/light switches				
Light fixtures				
Windows—aluminum/double hung/ casement/iron bar grille/other				
Fireplace				
Damper/firescreen/ firebricks/mortar & grout				
Free-standing fireplace				
Heating appliance/duct/ registers/thermostat				
Dining room				
Condition				
Walls/ceiling				
Floor—carpeted/hardwood/other				
Wall receptacle plug				
Outlets/light switches				
Light fixtures				
Windows—aluminum/double hung/ casement/other				
Fireplace				
Heating appliance/duct/thermostat				
Sliding glass door				
Safety tempered glass				
Operable				
Lock present				
Insulated				
Kitchen				
Condition				

S: *Satisfactory*   U: *Unsatisfactory*   NA: *Not applicable*

	S	U	NA	Comments
Kitchen, cont'd.				
Sink drainboard/backsplash				
Sink mortar/ceramic tiles				
Faucets				
Water pressure				
Pipes bang				
P trap				
Garbage disposal				
Stove—gas/electric				
Vent				
Connection				
Shut-off valve for gas stove				
Exhaust fan & hood				
Light fixtures				
Dishwasher				
Windows—aluminum/double hung/casement/other				
Walls—condition				
Ceiling—condition				
U-ground				
Wall receptacle plug				
Outlets/switches				
Heater duct				
Infestations—rodent/roach/other				
Family room				
Condition				
Walls/ceiling				
Floor—carpet/hardwood/other				
Wall receptacle plug				
Outlets/switches				
Light fixtures				
Windows—aluminum/double hung/casement/other				
Fireplace				
Damper/bricks/mortar				
Heating appliance/duct				

S: *Satisfactory*   U: *Unsatisfactory*   NA: *Not applicable*

	S	U	NA	Comments
Family room, cont'd.				
Sliding glass door				
Safety tempered glass				
Operable				
Lock present				
Insulated				
Master bedroom				
Condition				
Walls/ceiling				
Floor—carpet/hardwood/other				
Wall receptacle plug				
Outlets/switches				
Light fixtures				
Windows—aluminum/double hung/ casement/other				
Heating appliance/duct				
Closets				
Ceiling				
Attic access cover				
Insulation				
Bedroom #2				
Condition				
Walls/ceiling				
Floor—carpet/hardwood/other				
Wall receptacle plug				
Outlets/switches				
Light fixtures				
Windows—aluminum/double hung/ casement/other				
Heating appliance/duct				
Closets				
Hall				
Smoke detector				
Walls/ceiling				
Floor—carpet/hardwood/other				
Wall receptacle plug				

S: *Satisfactory*   U: *Unsatisfactory*   NA: *Not applicable*

	S	U	NA	Comments
Hall, cont'd.				
Outlets/switches				
Light fixtures				
Skylight				
Heating appliance/duct				
Closets				
Bathroom				
Walls/ceiling				
Floor—tile/linoleum/other				
Windows—aluminum/double hung/other				
U-ground				
GFI				
Wall receptacle plug				
Outlets/switches				
Light fixtures				
Heater duct				
Toilet				
Wash basin				
Faucets/P trap				
Secured to wall				
Shut-off handles				
Tub shower				
Curtain rod/shower/enclosure/other				
Tile/other				
Condition				
Faucet				
Mechanical fan				
Insulation				
Roof: inches of insulation				
Walls: inches of insulation				
Raised floor: inches of insulation				
Garage				
Attached/detached				
One-hour fire resistant wall next to living area				
Solid-core door				

S: *Satisfactory*   U: *Unsatisfactory*   NA: *Not applicable*

	S	U	NA	Comments
Garage, cont'd.				
Stairway railing				
Laundry tub—plastic/cement/other				
U-ground outlets/switches				
Heating system				
Wall furnace/floor furnace/forced air				
Air grilles clean				
Vent rises 1/4″ per foot				
Adequate combustion air				
Gas dryer				
Exhaust to exterior				
Cooling systems				
Clean				
Recently serviced				
Noisy/quiet				
Filters				
Connectors and accessibility				
Meets minimum heat requirements				
Utility room				
Condition				
Laundry tub—cement/plastic				
Tub stabilized/secured/ properly braced				
Separate 20-amp circuit for clothes washer				

S: *Satisfactory*   U: *Unsatisfactory*   NA: *Not applicable*

Building Permits

A property owner must obtain a local building permit if he or she wants to erect, construct, enlarge, alter, repair, move, remove, convert, or demolish any building or structure. The permit should be obtained before any construction work begins.

There are four basic permits: building permit (Fig. 92), plumbing permit, mechanical permit, and electrical permit. To obtain a permit, the property owner must file a written application; in many cases two sets of plans and specifications must accompany the application. Permit fees are based on the total value of the construction project. Large projects and those involving structural members require an additional fee to cover the checking of plans.

The general contractor for the project is responsible for obtaining all necessary permits. If a property owner acts as the general contractor, he or she must assume this responsibility. In addition, licensed subcontractors must obtain the relevant permits in their own names, but it is up to the general contractor to be sure that they do.

When you apply for a permit, you will be asked to sign a certificate stating that (1) you are the owner of the property on which the work will take place; (2) you will comply with all building, zoning, and fire codes; (3) the building department has no liability for the work done on the property—even if the department inspects and approves the completed work; and (4) all people you hire for the job will be adequately insured. In most cases the fee for the building permit will run no more than 7 percent of the cost of the work.

People sometimes fail to obtain permits because they are afraid that the inspectors will demand that certain other repairs be made to bring the building up to code, or that the inspection will result in higher property taxes. But failure to obtain a permit is illegal. And there are many benefits to obtaining the required permit:

- The building department will provide you with guidelines and procedures, as well as reference materials and referrals.

- The building department inspector may detect an existing hazard to your health and safety.

- By following the building code and zoning requirements, you will know that the construction work is safe and that you will not have to have the work redone.

- By using licensed contractors, all of whom carry workmen's compensation insurance, you limit your legal liability for on-the-job accidents.

- Code compliance and proof of completion may be required for refinancing the property.

- Code compliance offers assurance to future purchasers of the property.

Hiring a Contractor

The best way to select a reputable contractor is to ask friends or relatives for referrals. Also contact the local building department, Better Business Bureau, and any other agencies that have files on contractors' performance.

Take your plans and specifications to at least three different contractors and ask for written estimates. To avoid costly mistakes and misunderstandings, be clear about what work you want to have done and how much money you want to spend. If one estimate is substantially lower than the other two, ask the contractor to explain his bid.

Draw up a written agreement before any work begins. All agreements between you and the contractor should be *in writing*. Don't assume that any verbal agreements are valid—get everything in writing.

Before the contractor signs off on the project, look over the work together. Make sure that all building permits have been approved and that the building inspector has signed the final completion form. The completion date is very important; there are penalties for going over the date.

Many unlicensed contractors do good work, but if you hire an unlicensed contractor, you may be inviting trouble. For example, an unlicensed roofer may not have workmen's compensation insurance. If the roofer or an assistant gets hurt on the job, you could be sued for damages. In contrast, licensed contractors are required to be bonded by the state licensing board and carry workmen's compensation insurance.

Glossary

Accessory building	Structure supplementary to a main residential building, such as tool shed or garage.
Addition	A portion of a building added to the original structure; a synonym for *subdivision* in certain legal descriptions.
Air gap	A separation between any pipe or faucet conveying water and the flood-level rim of any plumbing receptacle.
Alcove	A recessed part or addition to a room.
Ampere	A measure of the rate of flow of electric current through wiring.
Anti-siphon valve	Valve on a lawn sprinkler that prevents the sprinkler water from backflowing into the main water supply.
Apartment	One or more rooms of a building used as a dwelling unit within a building containing at least one other unit used for the same purpose. Usually has, at the least, cooking facilities, a bathroom, and a place to sleep.
Apartment house	A building containing three or more separate dwelling units that are rented to tenants.
Arch	A concave curve span over a doorway or an entire room or building such as an arched ceiling or roof.
Asbestos	A fire- and heat-resistant material used in construction until the early 1970s, when it was discovered to pose health hazards.
Attic	The space under the roof of a structure but above the top story.
Baluster	The supporting poles of a handrail along a staircase.
Balustrade	A row of balusters topped by a rail, edging a balcony or a staircase.
Baseboard	Any board or molding covering an interior wall where it meets the floor.
Basement	The story of a building that is below ground level.
Bathroom	A room containing a toilet, sink, and bathtub or bathtub-shower combination.
Batt	An oblong blanket of fiberglass insulation.
Beam	A principal horizontal structural member used between posts, columns, or walls.

Bearing or wall partition   A wall that supports a vertical load such as the roof.

Blueprint   A detailed plan of a building used by construction workers. The name comes from the photographic process that produces the plan in white on a blue background.

Building code   A comprehensive set of laws that governs the construction and use of buildings, including design, materials, repair, remodeling, and the like. Statewide regulations may apply.

Building contract   A written contract between a property owner and a builder that sets forth the terms under which construction is to be undertaken.

Building paper   A waterproof heavy paper used in the construction of a roof or wall.

Building permit   A permit issued by a local government that allows the construction or remodeling of a building.

Built-up roofs   A flat or low-pitched roof covered by several layers of asphalt-saturated felts glued together with hot asphalt (tar) and surfaced with gravel or rocks.

Carport   A wall-less roofed shelter for a car.

Caulk   To seal a crack or joint, especially around a window or exterior door frame, with a water or airtight putty.

Cellar   A storage room or group of rooms, usually under a building.

Certificate of occupancy   A document issued by local building officials that indicates a multi-family building is up to code.

Check Valve   A valve that prevents backup of material in a pipe or other conduit.

Chimney   Any passage through which smoke from a fire passes. Most commonly a brick passage from a fireplace to the roof of a building.

Circuit analyzer   An electrical tester used to determine whether the polarity at an outlet is correct and whether the ground is properly wired and functioning.

Circuit breaker   An electrical device that shuts off the electric current when a circuit becomes overloaded. The circuit breaker can be reset by hand.

Cleanout plug   A threaded fitting in a pipe or fixture that provides access for cleaning or drainage.

Collar tie beam   A horizontal beam fastened above the lower ends of rafters.

Condominium   A structure of two or more units, the interior spaces of which are individually owned; the balance of the property (both land and building) is owned in common by all the owners of the individual units. The size of each unit is measured from the interior surfaces (exclusive of paint or other finishes) of the exterior walls, floors, and ceiling. The balance of the property is called the common area.

Conduit, electrical	A rigid or flexible metal pipe through which electrical wiring is installed.
Crawl space	A space between the ground and the first floor of a house that allows access for repair of utilities that run under the house.
Cripple wall	*See* Pony wall.
Damper	An adjustable plate in the flue of a fireplace or furnace that is used to control the draft from the flames.
Deck	Any flat outdoor surface that is not enclosed, such as a flat area on a roof or the roof of a porch.
Dielectric (union)	A type of connector that insulates two different types of metal pipe to prevent electrolysis.
Diversion valve	Valve in a septic tank system that allows the user to alternate leach lines.
Double glazing	Insulated window pane formed of two thicknesses of glass with a sealed air space between them.
Double-hung window	A window that opens vertically from the top and bottom, containing two separate sashes, each supported by cords and weights.
Double lugging	Running two circuits off a single lug.
Downspout	A pipe leading from the gutters of a roof to the ground and, usually, into a sewer or away from the building.
Downspout strap	A piece of metal that secures the downspout to the eaves or wall of a building.
Drainage	The gradual flowing of liquids off a surface. Any system to remove liquid waste or rainwater by channeling its flow to a designated area.
Dry wall	Materials used for interior wall covering that do not need to be mixed with water before application. Also called gypsum board, wallboard, or sheetrock.
Ducts	Any conduit for hot air, gas, water, electrical wiring, etc.
Duplex	A building that contains two dwelling units. Most commonly the units are side by side, with a common wall and roof.
Dwelling unit	Any building or portion of a building that contains facilities for sleeping, eating, cooking, and sanitation.

DWV   Domestic waste-vent system, also called sewage and relief vent piping.

Eaves   The margin or lower part of a roof that projects beyond an exterior wall.

EMT   Electrical metallic steel tubing—a very light rigid conduit.

Fascia   A flat horizontal member of a cornice placed in a vertical position.

Fill-type insulation   Loose insulating material that is applied by hand or mechanically blown into wall spaces.

Firebrick   Special clay brick that can be exposed to extremely high temperatures without damage. Used in furnaces, fireplaces, and similar high-temperature areas.

Flashing   Sheet metal or similar materials, used at different points in a structure to prevent water seepage, such as around vent pipes or chimneys.

Floor furnace   A ductless furnace placed directly below a floor that transmits heat only through a grille in the floor.

Floor joists   A framing piece that rests on the outer foundation walls and interior beams or girders.

Flue   The opening or passageway in a chimney through which smoke, gases, etc., pass from a building. Any opening or passageway for the elimination of gases or fumes.

Footing   A footlike projection at the base of a foundation wall, column, pier, etc., used to secure, support, and help eliminate settling or shifting.

Forced-air furnace   A furnace that has a fan or blower which forces warm air through the ducts.

Foundation   The part of a building, usually below ground level, that supports the superstructure.

Framing   The wood structure of a building that provides its strength and shape; includes exterior and interior walls, floor, roof, and ceilings.

Furring   Finish material applied to a wall to smooth or level the surface for lathing or plastering.

Fuse   A short plug in an electric panel box that interrupts an electrical circuit when it becomes overloaded.

Garage   A building adjacent or attached to a residence that is used to store or repair motor vehicles.

Girder   A large or principal beam used to support concentrated loads or weight at particular points along its length.

Ground-fault circuit interrupter	A device that interrupts an electric circuit when the incoming and outgoing currents are not equal.
Gutter	A channel along the eaves that directs rainwater to a downspout. Also the channel formed by the meeting of the street and curb, where rainwater runs to the sewer.
Habitable room	A room such as a kitchen, bedroom, or dining room, as opposed to bathrooms, closets, hallways, and similar spaces.
Hardwood	The close-grained wood from broadleafed trees such as oak or maple.
Header	Horizontal structural member that supports the load over an opening such as a window or door. Also called a *lintel*.
Hearth	The stone or brick floor extending in front and to the sides of the fireplace opening.
Income property	Property that produces income for its owner, usually from rental. May also include property not entirely owner occupied.
Insulation	Material high in resistance to heat transmission that is placed in structures to reduce the rate of heat gain or loss.
Joist	One of the series of parallel framing members used to support the floor and ceiling; joists are supported in turn by larger beams, girders, or bearing walls.
Junction box	A device in which wires are spliced to bring various circuits together.
Knob-and-tube wiring	Oldest type of electrical wiring. The knobs serve as insulators, and the ceramic tubes isolate the wiring from neighboring wood.
Lath	A building material of wood, metal, gypsum, or insulating board fastened to the frame of building to act as a base for a plaster finish.
Lavatory	A basin or sink for washing one's hands and face. Also a room containing a sink and a toilet.
Leach line	A gravel-filled subsurface trench extending from a septic tank. Liquid wastes are absorbed into the leach line's soil.
Linoleum	A floor covering used in heavily trafficked areas (kitchens, bathrooms, entrances, etc.) made of cork, linseed oil, resins, and pigments on a canvas or burlap backing, and applied from a roll.
Load-bearing wall	A wall capable of supporting weight.
Main circuit	The principal circuit that feeds electrical current into smaller circuits (branches) for distribution.
Mantel	A shelf above a fireplace; the decorative framework around a fireplace.

Moisture barrier   Treated paper, plastic, or metal that retards or bars water vapor, used to keep moisture from passing into walls or floors.

Mudsill   The lowest horizontal timber of a wall, usually placed in or on the ground in older buildings; on top of the foundation in buildings with foundations.

Nonbearing partition   A wall extending from floor to ceiling that supports no load other than its own weight; designed to separate rooms. Can be knocked down without jeopardizing the safety or strength of the structure.

Nonmetallic sheathed cable   Electric wiring that has two or more insulated wires and one bare ground wire encased in a plastic or fabric sheath. Often called *romex* or *NM*.

Ordinance   A law or statute enacted by the legislative body of a municipal corporation or a county.

Parapet   A low wall or barrier at the edge of a balcony or roof.

Pitch   The angle of slope of a roof.

Planning commission   A board of a city, county, or similar local government, entrusted with the approval of proposed building projects. Usually its decisions must be confirmed by a higher board, such as a council.

Plenum   A chamber that can serve as a distribution area for heating or cooling systems, generally located between a false ceiling and the actual ceiling.

Plumbing   The pipes and fixtures necessary for the flow of water to a building and the flow of sanitary waste from the building.

Polarity   The electrical charge, either positive or negative, of an electric service terminal.

Pony wall   A short wall built upon the foundation of a house that produces a high crawl space. Also called a *cripple wall*.

Porch   A covered entrance to a building; a room that opens to the outside, often having no walls or glass or screened walls.

Purlin   A beam that runs the length of a roof and supports rafters at a point near the midspan of the rafters.

R value   A measurement of a material's resistance to transmitting heat; the higher the R value, the better the insulation provided.

Radiant heat   Coils of electricity, hot water, or steam pipes embedded in floors, ceilings, or walls to heat rooms.

Rafter   Load-bearing timbers of a roof. Flat roof rafters are usually called *joists*.

Reconditioning	Restoring a property to a good condition without changing its plan or character, as distinguished from remodeling. Also called *renovation* or *rehabilitation*.
Rehabilitation	Synonymous with *reconditioning*, except when used in connection with urban renewal, at which time it encompasses all types of changes, including structural and even street changes.
Remodeling	Improving a structure by changing its plan, characteristics, or function, as opposed to *reconditioning*.
Ridge	The highest point of a hip or gable roof.
Ridgeboard	The area where two sloping surfaces meet.
Riser	The upright piece of a stair step, from tread to tread.
Romex	*See* Nonmetallic sheathed cable.
Sash	The moveable part of a window—the frame in which panes of glass are set in a window or door.
Scupper	An opening in the side of a parapet on a flat roof.
Setback ordinance	Zoning ordinance that regulates the distance from the lot line to the point where improvements may be constructed.
Sheathing paper	A moisture resistant building material used in wall, floor, and roof construction.
Sheetrock	A plasterboard compound of a core of gypsum between two sheets of heavy paper.
Shingles	Roof or wall surfacing of overlapping small sheets of wood, slate, tile, asphalt, or other waterproof material.
Siding	The finish covering of the outside wall of a frame building. Types available include aluminum, vinyl, and wood.
Skylight	A window in a roof or ceiling.
Slab	Concrete floor placed directly on earth or a gravel base, and usually about 4 inches thick.
Soffit	Undersurface of an arch, overhang, stairway, or other such part of a building.
Spark arrester	A wire mesh device placed atop a chimney to prevent embers from blowing out onto the roof.
Sprinkler system	In reference to residential property, a system of pipes under a lawn used for watering the grass. In commercial or industrial property, a system of ceiling pipes and valves sensitive to ambient temperatures that when activated automatically sprinkles water or a chemical fire retardant.
Stucco	A wet plaster finish, specifically designed for exterior use; popular as an outside wall surface in warm, dry climates.

Studs   A vertical structural member of a wall to which horizontal pieces are nailed. Studs are spaced either 16 inches or 24 inches apart.

Thermostat   The part of a heating or air conditioning system that controls the heating or cooling unit in order to bring ambient air to a preset temperature.

Threshold   A wooden or metal strip under an outside door; the entrance to a building.

Townhouse   Originally a house in a city as opposed to a country estate. More recently, a type of row house.

Trap   A bend in a water pipe that retains water in order to prevent gases from the plumbing system from backing into the house.

Tread   The horizontal part of a stair step.

Truss   An assembly of beams that forms a rigid support for a roof or other structure.

Valley   The depression at the meeting point of two roof slopes; provides proper water runoff from the roof.

Vapor barrier Material such as paper, metal, or paint used to prevent vapor from passing from rooms into the outside walls.

Vent pipe   A pipe installed to provide a flow of air to or from a drainage system or to provide for circulation of air within a plumbing system.

Weep hole   A small hole in a wall that permits water to drain off.

Window sill   The bottom framing member of a window casing.

Zip cord   Light-gauge electrical wire; poses a serious fire hazard when used to run additional outlets or appliances.

Zoning   The division of a city or county by legislative regulations into areas (zones) distinguished by the permissible uses for real property.

Zoning Ordinance A law, usually at the city or county level, controlling the use of land and construction of improvements in a given area (zone).

Bibliography

BOOKS

Bucholtz, John J. *The Consumers Stucco Handbook.* 5178 Moorpark Ave., San Jose, California 95129, Perfection Publishers, 1979.

Hemp, Peter A. *The Straight Poop: A Plumber's Tattler.* Berkeley, California: Ten Speed Press, 1986.

Hoffman, George. *Don't Go Buy Appearances: A Manual for House Inspection.* Revised edition. Corte Madera, California: Woodward Books, 1978.

Hunter, Steve. *1980 Home Inspection Workbook.* Maplewood, New Jersey: Hammond, 1980.

International Conference of Building Officials. *Uniform Building Code.* Whittier, California, 1985.

International Conference of Building Officials. *Dwelling Construction under the Uniform Building Code.* Whittier, California, 1976.

International Conference of Building Officials. *Uniform Housing Code.* Whittier, California, 1988.

International Conference of Building Officials. *Uniform Mechanical Code.* Whittier, California, 1988.

International Conference of Building Officials. *National Electric Code.* Whittier, California, 1987.

International Conference of Plumbing and Mechanical Officials. *Uniform Plumbing Code.* Los Angeles, 1988.

Jones, Robert, and Monte Burch. *Fireplaces: Adding, Improving, Heat Saving Systems, Wood Stoves.* New York: Macmillan, 1980.

Le Patner, Barry, and Sidney M. Johnson. *Structural and Foundation Failures.* New York: Macmillan, 1965.

Sunset Books. *Basic Home Wiring.* 5th edition. Palo Alto, California: Lane Publishing, 1980.

Sunset Books. *Roofing and Siding, Do-It-Yourself.* Palo Alto, California: Lane Publishing, 1981.

Yanov, Peter. *Peace of Mind in Earthquake Country.* San Francisco: Chronicle Books, 1980.

MAGAZINE ARTICLES

Hoffman, George.   "Money Talks." *McCalls*, October 1979.

Miller, Peter.   "How to Avoid Doghouses—Inspecting Homes Before You Buy." *Washingtonian*, February 1981.

"Can That House Pass Inspection?"   *Better Homes and Gardens*, September 1980.

PAMPHLETS

"Landlord Tenant."   Pamphlet available from Department of Consumer Affairs, 1020 N Street, Sacramento, CA 95814. 1984.

Building Officials and Code Administrators International, Inc.   "You Can Build It." Available from International Congress of Building Officials, 5360 South Workman Mill Road, Whittier, CA 90601.

Department of Agriculture.   "Finding and Keeping a Healthy House." Available from Government. Printing Office, Stock No: 001-000-03263-1, $3.25.

Department of Consumer Affairs, California Contractors' State License Board.   "Blueprint for Building Quality." Available from Department of Consumer Affairs, Contractors State License Board, 1020 N Street, Sacramento, California 95814.

Division of Agricultural Sciences, University of California. "So You've Just Had a Structural Pest Control Inspection." University of California Extension Service Leaflet #2999. Available from U.C. Extension Service, Berkeley, CA 94720.

Energy Conservation Center, Pacific Gas & Electric Company.   "A Guide to Solar Control and Insulating Glass Products, Windows."   Available from San Francisco, CA 94106.

Energy Conservation Center, Pacific Gas & Electric Company.   "Insulate—Save Energy." Available from San Francisco, CA 94106.

U.S. Consumer Product Safety Commission.   "Asbestos in the Home." Superintendent of Documents, U.S. Government Printing Office, Washington, D.C. 20402.

U.S. Consumer Product Safety Commission.   "Was Your Home Built After 1964? Do You Have an Electrical System with Aluminum Wiring?" Revised April 1980. Available from: U.S. Consumer Product Safety Commission, Washington, D.C. 20207.

Index

MORE BOOKS ON BUILDING AND HOUSECRAFTS

Before You Build
A Preconstruction Guide
by Robert Roskind

A comprehensive guide to everything you need to know before building a house. Detailed instructions and checklists cover everything from buying the land to insurance and financing to deciphering building codes.

$11.95   200 pages

Building Your Own House
Part I
by Robert Roskind

Starting with a discussion of design and planning, safety tips, and a complete checklist of tools, this volume takes the novice builder step by step from foundations through framing. Illustrated with diagrams, drawings, and hundreds of photos.

$17.95   448 pages

Building Your Own House
Part II
by Robert Roskind

Takes up where the first volume left off, guiding the builder through everything they need to know for finishing an interior. Also handy as a remodelling guide.

$17.95   288 pages

Rehab Right
by Helene Kaplan Prentice,
Blair Prentice, and the
City of Oakland
Planning Department

A guide to restoring just about any house built since the late nineteenth century.
"This book is a must-have for serious
—or not-so-serious—rehabbers."
—*Home Magazine*
$9.95   144 pages

Shelter
edited by Lloyd Kahn

Between a scrapbook and a reference book, SHELTER is a celebration of simple and beautiful dwellings, natural materials, and human resourcefulness. Over 1,000 photos, hundreds of drawings, anecdotes, and building tips.

$16.95   176 pages

Cohousing: A Contemporary
Approach to Housing Ourselves
by Kathryn McCamant
& Charles Durrett

The first book about an innovative and successful form of housing already popular in Europe. Based on the study of over 50 cohousing communities, it offers a new solution to the urban housing shortage. Color photos.

$19.95   208 pages

The Handyman's Book
by Paul N. Hasluck

A reprint of the 1903 classic—the most exhaustive treatment of woodworking in its day. Over 2,500 illustrations.

$9.95   800 pages

The Straight Poop
A Plumber's Tattler
by Peter Hemp

A professional plumber's guide to dealing with common plumbing problems. Heavily illustrated, this book can save even the most inexperienced person time, effort, and a lot of money.

$9.95   176 pages

When ordering please include an additional $1 per book for shipping and handling. Contact us for bulk shipping rates.

Ten Speed Press
Box 7123, Berkeley, California 94707